Cardozo on the Parashah
Bereshit | Genesis

With Questions to Ponder from the
David Cardozo Academy Think Tank

Kasva Press

St. Paul / Alfei Menashe

Copyright © 2019 by Nathan Lopes Cardozo

All rights reserved. No part of this book may be reproduced or transmitted in any form or by any means whatsoever without express written permission from the author, except in the case of brief quotations embodied in critical articles and reviews.

Cover photo by Claudia Kamergorodski

Kasva Press
Alfei Menashe, Israel
St. Paul, Minnesota

www.kasvapress.com
info@kasvapress.com

Cardozo on the Parashah

ISBN: 978-1-948403-10-8 (Hardcover)

M 10 9 8 7 6 5 4 3 2 1

This book was made possible by the generosity
of the Babaoff Family, Los Angeles, California.

---

*In honor of our parents,
Azar and Mehdi (Meir) Babaoff.
Thank you for instilling in us the love of
reading and learning.*

Kambiz and Lily Babaoff

Contents

Foreword — xi
Preface — xiii

Encountering Torah
The Unavoidable and Disturbing Text — 3

Encountering Bereshit
The Purpose of Sefer Bereshit: Restraining Religious Law — 15

Bereshit
The Unknowable, Loving, and Aggravating God — 29
The Lessons of Religious Optimism — 39
Freud's Subconscious Discovery of God — 45

Noah
God and Natural Disasters — 51
The Idolatry of Theodicy — 57
Spinoza's Blunder and Noah's Misguided Religiosity — 63

Lech Lecha
Human Autonomy and Divine Commandment — 73
Circumcision: Why Risk Your Child's Well Being? — 81

Vayera
Our Struggle with God's Goodness — 93
The Religious Scandal of Akedat Yitzhak and the Tragedy of God — 101

Haye Sara
Leadership and Captainship — 111

The Curse of Religious Boredom	115
How Old Would You Be If You Didn't Know Your Age?	123

Toldot

Avraham and Individuality; Old Age and Facelifts	131
Even God Admits Mistakes	137

Vayetze

The Art of Prayer	147
The Danger of Religion	155

Vayishlach

Amalek and a Warning Against Injustice	165
Remembering Who We Are	173

Vayeshev

The Many-Colored Garment	181
Freedom of Will and Determinism: A Daring Midrash	187

Miketz

Divine Emanations and Human Responses	195
The Tragedy of the Tzaddik	201

Vayigash

Generational Awareness	211
Arguing Against Oneself: Yosef's Revenge	221

Vayechi

The Great Educational Challenge	231
The Number of the Generations before Him	239

Glossary	245
Acknowledgments	251

If I only believe what I understand then
my faith is no larger than my head.

> Godfried Bomans
> Celebrated Dutch Author
> 1913-1971

Cardozo on the Parashah
Bereshit

With Questions to Ponder from the David Cardozo Academy Think Tank

Foreword

WHILE I TAKE full responsibility for the text of the Torah which I dictated to my servant Moshe on Mount Sinai, I am not responsible for the interpretations which over the thousands of years have been written by some of My most devoted followers.

It is true that I gave them permission to interpret based on the principle of "Lo BaShamayim Hi" (Devarim 30:12), the Torah is no longer in Heaven. I have indeed asked them to participate in exploring My Torah and "turn it over and over because everything is in it" as Ben Bag Bag said in Pirkei Avot (5:22). But sometimes I have been surprised, and even taken aback, by what they wrote in My name about My Torah, and wondered how they ever came to such outrageous ideas!

This is even more the case with Nathan Lopes Cardozo. After much deliberation, and after reading the questions by the members of the David Cardozo Think Tank, who at least take My side, I have reluctantly given permission to Kasva Press to publish his interpretations, although I have great doubts he got it right.

My permission to publish this book is therefore only valid as long as Cardozo is ashamed of some of its content.

אחתום אשר אחתום!

God

aka. Hashem, Adonai, HaMakom, HaKadosh Baruch Hu,
Elohim, El, Ribbono shel Olam, Tzvaot, Shadai, Ein Sof....
Author of *The Five Books of Moses*, Sinai. Holy Publishers,
2448 since the Creation of the Universe.

Preface

THIS IS THE first of several volumes discussing certain halachic-moral and philosophical topics within Parashat HaShavua, the weekly Shabbat readings of the Torah in the Synagogue. This series will be followed by one on the Jewish Festivals, which I have written or spoken about in the last ten years.

This volume discusses only topics which came to my mind in relationship to the book of Bereshit/Genesis. Some are deep, others controversial and perhaps shocking to some mainstream religious or non-religious people. Others are just unusual but sweet.

There is no consistency among these essays. All topics stand on their own (with one or two exceptions) and do not have to be read in any particular order.

The essays were first published as "Thoughts to Ponder" which I write every week for the David Cardozo Academy website. Many of them have appeared in the *Times of Israel* and the *Jerusalem Post* as well as other Jewish or non-Jewish journals, papers, and books.

I did not write these essays with the purpose of persuading people to agree with me, but with the aim that they would become topics of (fierce) debate at the Jewish Shabbat table.

But I also hope that they will be read at Sunday assemblies in churches and other houses of worship, and even in secular gatherings or at family get-togethers. For the benefit of non-Hebrew speakers, Hebrew words are defined in a glossary at the end of the book.

There are conflicting ideas among the essays, reflecting the rabbinic tradition (Talmud: Eruvin 13b) that religious disagreements are all rooted in the word of God, Whose words cannot be captured in any final truth. I am not even sure I always agree with myself. If I did, I would be ashamed of myself as it would mean that I am no longer spiritually alive and that I believe that the word of God has been exhausted. That would be the greatest insult to God Himself.

Having said all this, the reader should be aware that my observations are deeply rooted in the Jewish tradition, which I have chosen to be the spiritual guide in my life and that of my family.

I thank Urim Publications in Jerusalem, especially Tzvi Maor, for allowing me to use some of the essays which were earlier published in several of my earlier books.

The publication of this book and those that follow in the series was made possible by Kam and lily Babaoff of Los Angeles. Chazak Baruch to them, not only for their financial support but also for their ongoing encouragement.

I also wish to thank Rony and Toby Hersh of New York for all their support. Thank you also to Joseph and Renée Krant in Amsterdam and many other Dutch friends. I also thank Rabbi and Mrs Zeev (Wim) van Dijk for their great friendship, as well as Benja and Grace Philipson, previously of Haarlem and now Jerusalem.

As always I thank my late parents, Jacob and Bertha Lopes Cardozo, my brother Dr. Jacques Eduard Lopes Cardozo, may he live long together with his family, and my late parents-in-law Grisha and Rosa Gnesin, who encouraged and supported me while studying the Jewish Tradition and growing in wisdom.

Preface

The late Aron and Betsy Spijer and the Board of the Dutch "Spijer Foundation," Dr. Leo Delfgaauw, Dr. Hans Wijnfeldt and Mr. Eldad Eitje have been responsible for much of my achievements and have enabled me to teach, publish and run the David Cardozo Academy.

Special thanks should be extended to my dear friend Mrs. Jenny Weil who recently passed away and her husband Max Weil, may he live a long life together with all his family, for constantly supporting all my efforts.

Thanks are due to the Think Tank of the David Cardozo Academy (run by Yael Shahar and Jonathan Rossner and formerly by Yael Unterman and Yael Valier) which is constantly challenging me to come up with new ideas, some of which are found in this book.

The Boards of the Israeli Ohr Aaron Foundation together with our foundation in England, especially Mr. David Yamin-Joseph, the American and Canadian Foundations are all the be thanked.

Special thanks to my editor and good friend Chana Shapiro who makes sure my English is as flawless as it humanly can be.

Very special thanks to (Rabbi) Yehudah Behr Zirkin for having gone through all the essays, put them together in order of the weekly portion of the Torah (Parashat Hashavua) and carefully checked all the sources. A major undertaking!

Chazak baruch to my secretary Esther Peterman who takes care of our administration and all other matters related to our Academy. Also thanks to Ilana Sinclair and Sarah Landman for all their help.

Thank you also to Yael Shahar who has been sending my weekly Thoughts to Ponder via Internet to thousands of people. She and her husband Don at Kasva Press have done an outstanding job at publishing this series!

Especially, thanks to my children, children-in-law, grandchildren, and great grandchildren who give me much joy and who are a constant source of inspiration. Their commitment to Judaism is my life-line.

Last but not least, my dear wife Frijda Rachel who endures my long hours at my office, writing and teaching, with great patience and supports me in every way possible. Being married to her for 52 years is a great blessing. May it continue for a long time! Not one of my many books would ever have appeared without her help.

Above all, thanks to the Lord of the Universe who made all this possible.

To Him all praise,

Nathan Lopes Cardozo
Jerusalem,
Sivan 5779/ June 2019

Encountering Torah

The Unavoidable and Disturbing Text

TORAH STUDY HAS become nearly impossible, and the problem lies not with the Torah but with the reader. Reading the text requires courage — courage not to open the Book and start reading, but courage to confront *oneself*. Learning Torah requires human authenticity; it means standing in front of a mirror and asking yourself the daunting question of who you *really* are, without masks and artificialities. Unfortunately, that is one of the qualities we, in modern times, have lost. We have convinced ourselves that we must be intellectuals, removed from subjectivity and bowing only to scientific investigation. Consequently, we have disconnected from our true selves. Because we humans are a bundle of emotions, passions and subjectivities, we cannot escape our inner world, much as we would like to.

Still, we formulate ideas. We may proclaim the rights of the spirit, but our ideas enter only our books and discussions, not our lives. They float around in our heads, rather than walking with us into the inner chambers of our daily existence. They don't enter our trivial moments, but rather stand as monuments — impressive, but far removed.

People are no longer able to struggle with this inner Self, and therefore cannot deal with the biblical text. It stares them in the face, and they are terrified by the confrontation. All they can do is deny it, so that they may escape from themselves. Since they know that they must come to terms with themselves before they come to terms with the Book, they cannot negate it or disagree with it, as this requires them to deny something that they don't even know exists.

Does that mean that these people are not religious? Not at all. Even religious people are detached from the spirit. They have elevated religion to such a level that its influence on their everyday life, in the here and now, has been lost. It is found on the top floor of their spiritual house, with its own very special atmosphere. It has become compartmentalized. But the intention of Torah is exactly the reverse. Its words, events and commandments are placed in the *midst* of the people, enveloped in history and worldly matters. What happens there does not take place in a vacuum, but in the harshness of human reality. Most of the Torah deals with the natural course of a person's life. Only sporadic miracles allow us to hear the murmurs from another world that exists beyond. These moments remind us that God is, after all, the only real entity in all of existence. But the Torah is the story of how God exists among mortal human beings, with their ordinary troubles and joys. It is not the story of God in heaven, but of God in human history and personal encounter.

THE TEXT IS THE AUTHOR OF THE PEOPLE

The art of biblical interpretation is far more than just knowing how to give expression to the deeper meaning of the text. It is, after all, impossible to treat the biblical text as one would any other classical work. This is because the people of Israel, according to Jewish tradition, are not the authors of this text. Rather, the text is the author of the people. As a covenant between God and humankind, the text is what brought the people into being. Moreover, despite the fact that the people have often violated the commanding voice of this text, it created the specific and unique identity of the Jewish nation.

That is precisely why reading the text is not like reading a conventional literary work. It requires a reading-art, which unveils the unfolding of the essence and nature of a living people struggling with life and God's commandments.

This reading calls for a totally different kind of comprehension, one that must reflect a particular thought process and attitude on the part of the student. George Steiner expressed this well when he wrote:

> The script...is a contract with the inevitable. God has, in the dual sense of utterance and of binding affirmation, "given His word," His *Logos* and His bond, to Israel. It cannot be broken or refuted.[1]

The text, then, must be approached in a way that reflects a human commitment to ensure that it indeed will not be broken or refuted. This has become a great challenge to modern biblical interpretation. Many scholars and thinkers have been asking whether the unparalleled calamity of the Holocaust did not create a serious existential crisis in which the text, by definition, has been invalidated. Can we still speak about a working covenant by which God promised to protect His people, after six million Jews — including 1.5 million children — lost their lives within a span of five years, under the cruelest of circumstances?

The reason for raising this question is not just because the covenant appears to have been broken, but also because history — and specifically Jewish history — was always seen as a *living commentary* on the biblical text. The text gave significance to history and simultaneously took on its religious meaning.

Can the text still be used in that sense, or has it lost its significance because history violated the criteria for its proper and covenantal elucidation?

Not for nothing have modern scholars suggested that there is a need, post-Holocaust, to liberate ourselves from this covenantal text in favor of shaping our destiny and history in totally secular

---

1. George Steiner, "Our Homeland, the Text," in *The New Salmagundi Reader*, eds. Robert Boyers and Peggy Boyers (Syracuse: Syracuse University Press, 1996), 107.

terms. The Holocaust proved, they believe, that we have only ourselves to rely on, and even the return to Israel is to be understood as a secular liberation of the *galut* experience.

New commentary

It is in this context that "commentary" needs to take on a new challenge: to show not only how the covenant, as articulated in the text, has not been broken or refuted, but how in fact it is fully capable of dealing with the new post-Holocaust conditions of secularity.

Without falling victim to apologetics, biblical interpretation will have to offer a novel approach to dealing with the Holocaust experience in a full religious setting, based on the text and taking it beyond its limits. It will have to respond to the fact that God is the most tragic figure in all of history, making our lives sometimes sublime and other times disastrous. The biblical text is there to tell us how to live with this God and try to see meaning behind the absurdity of the situation.

But above all, modern commentary must make sure that the Torah speaks to the atheist and the agnostic, for they need to realize that the text is replete with examples of sincere deniers and doubters who struggled all their lives with great existential questions. The purpose is not to bring the atheists and agnostics back to the faith, but to show that *one can be religious while being an agnostic and perhaps even an atheist*; to make people aware that it is impossible to live without embarking on a search for meaning, whether one finds it or not. It is the search that is important; the end result much less so. Throughout the ages, the art has been to refrain from throwing such a pursuit on the dunghill of history. The struggle of *homo religiosus* is of the greatest importance to the atheist.

That many secular people no longer read the Torah is an enormous tragedy. The Torah is too important to be left to the believer.

The beauty of day-to-day life takes on a different and higher meaning through the Torah, and that can evoke in atheists a faintly mystical anticipation, which they can experience when they are alone or when they watch a sunset at the beach. A voice is born, and it speaks to them; they feel a melancholy that calls forth something far away and beyond. They happen upon a situation that suddenly throws them over the edge, and they get taken in by the experience of a loftier existence. They realize that the god they were told to believe in is not the God of the Torah. The latter is a God with Whom one argues; a God Who is criticized and Who wants human beings to search, even if it results in their denial of Him.

This issue is related to other crucial problems. Surveying Jewish history, we see drastic changes in how the biblical text was encountered. In the beginning, it was *heard* and not written. At first, Moshe received the Torah through the spoken Word: "The *Word* is very near to you; it is in your mouth and in your heart, for you to carry out."[2] God may be unimaginably far away, but His voice is heard nearby and it is the only way to encounter Him.

At a later stage, the Word evolved into a written form. Once this happened, there was a process by which the spoken Word was slowly silenced and gradually replaced by the written Word. With the eclipse of prophecy, God's Word was completely silenced and could then only be *read*. The Word, therefore, became frozen and ran the risk of becoming stagnant. At that stage, it was necessary to unfreeze the Word, which became the great task of the Sages and commentaries throughout the following centuries.

Relevance and eternity

Subsequently, a third element gained dominance. The text must be relevant to the generations that study it, while at the same time

---

2. *Devarim* 30:14.

remaining eternal. Commentators throughout the ages have struggled with this problem. How does one preserve the eternity of the Word and simultaneously make it relevant to a specific moment in time? Many commentators were children of their time and clearly read the text through the prism of the period in which they lived. The perspective of eternity thus became critical. It was often pushed to the background so as to emphasize the great message for the present. Much of the aspect of eternity was thereby compromised, causing a few to wonder how eternal this text really is.

Other commentators wrote as if nothing had happened in Jewish history. This reflected the remarkable situation of the Jewish people in *galut*: its a-historicity. After the destruction of the Temple, Jewish history came to a standstill. While much happened, with dire consequences for the Jews, they essentially lived their lives outside the historical framework of natural progress. It became a period of existential waiting, with the Jewish people anticipating the moment when they would once again enter history. This eventually came about with the establishment of the State of Israel in 1948.

Inevitably, then, some commentators wrote their exegeses in a historical vacuum. They hardly emphasized the relevance of biblical texts to a particular generation. Therefore, students were often confronted with a dual sentiment. While dazzled by a commentator's brilliant insight, they were forced to ask: So what? What is the implication of the interpretation for me, at this moment in time? Here we encounter a situation in which relevance is sacrificed for the sake of eternity.

With the return of the Jewish people to their ancestral homeland, Jews are confronted with an unprecedented situation, which has serious consequences for biblical commentary. Due to a very strong trend toward secularism, caused by the Holocaust, as well as other factors, the issue of relevance versus eternity has become greatly magnified.

Today, more than ever before, there exists a greater and more pressing need to show the relevance of the text. The radical changes in Jewish history call for a bold and novel way of understanding the text as a living covenant. At the same time, the drastic secularization of world Jewry and Israeli thinking requires a completely new approach to presenting the reader with the possibility of the Torah's eternity. With minor exceptions, the religious world has not come forward with an adequate response.

Innovation in receptivity

Most worrisome is the fact that the majority of Jewish commentaries published today in Orthodox circles are compilations and anthologies of earlier authorities, and do not open new vistas. It is as if original interpretations are no longer possible. The words of God are treated as if they have been exhausted. This clearly reflects either a fear of anything new, or an inability to come up with fresh and far-reaching ideas. This phenomenon has overtaken a good part of the Orthodox scholarly world. Jewish commentary is becoming more and more about writing glosses upon glosses, instead of creating new insights into the living covenant with God.

No doubt, not every person is equipped with the knowledge and creativity needed to undertake the task. Years of learning are an absolute requirement before one can make a genuine contribution in this field. Still, one must be aware of the danger of "over-knowledge." When students are overwhelmed by the interpretations of others, they may quite well become imprisoned by them and lose the art of thinking independently. Instead of becoming a vehicle to look for new ideas, their knowledge becomes detrimental.

What is required is *innovation in receptivity*, where fresh ideas can grow in the minds of those willing to think creatively about the classical sources, without being hampered by preconceived notions. Only then will we see novel approaches to our biblical tradition that will stand up to the challenges of our time.

Questions to Ponder
from the DCA Think Tank

1. To what extent do you agree or disagree with the suggestion "one can be religious while being an agnostic and perhaps even an atheist"? How might one define "religious" in the context of atheism — meaning, what actions, beliefs, thoughts, *weltanschauung*, etc. would characterize an atheist as "religious"?

2. The essay emphasizes the need for "innovation in receptivity, where fresh ideas can grow in the minds of those willing to think creatively about the classical sources, without being hampered by preconceived notions." What cultural, societal, educational, and political changes must occur in the secular Israeli community for that need to be met? What changes must occur in the religious Israeli community? Where are you personally in this picture?

3. What factors, beyond the Holocaust, played a role in the loss of creativity with regard to the traditional sources? To what extent did the broad phenomenon of secularization in the modern era play a role? Did the rise of the non-Orthodox movements contribute to this phenomenon? If so, how?

4. Can you think of practical steps that can be taken in advancing this creativity that will help generate relevance on the one hand, while preserving the sense of eternity on the other? To what extent can the dramatic (albeit gradual) transformations that led from biblical to rabbinic Judaism during the second temple period be repeated today? Might the rapid pace of technological developments where transformational processes are, perhaps, more transparent influence the development of religion too?

Encountering Bereshit

The Purpose of Sefer Bereshit:

Restraining Religious Law[1]

HALACHA, JEWISH LAW, is in trouble. More and more of the unacceptable is being done and said in its name. Besides causing infinite damage to Judaism's great message, it is a terrible desecration of God's name. And all of this is seen and heard by millions of Gentiles watching television, browsing websites, or listening to the radio. Many are repelled when they witness horrible scenes in which Jews attack each other in the name of Halacha. Media outlets around the world portray religious Jews in the most distressing ways. While it cannot be denied that antisemitism plays a role and tends to blow the picture out of proportion, the unfortunate fact is that much of it is based on truth. Non-Jews are dumbfounded when they read that leading rabbis make the most shocking comments, thereby demonstrating gross arrogance and discrimination. Even worse, many of them read about rabbinical decisions that seem to lack all moral integrity.

In 1995, Yigal Amir assassinated Prime Minister Yitzhak Rabin in the name of Halacha, claiming that the prime minister was a *rodef* (someone who is attempting or planning to murder) because he brought all of Israel's citizens into mortal danger by participating in the 1993 Oslo accords. Amir believed that the

---

1. This essay was published in Nathan Lopes Cardozo, *Jewish Law as Rebellion: A Plea for Religious Authenticity and Halachic Courage* (Jerusalem: Urim Publications, 2018), chap. 22.

prime minister therefore deserved the death penalty according to Jewish Law.

In 1994, Baruch Goldstein killed twenty-nine Arabs in the Cave of Machpela because he believed that Halacha obligated him to create havoc in order to stop Arab terror attacks, which had already killed thousands of Jews.[2]

Minorities such as the LGBT community are being insulted by powerful rabbis who seem to be ignorant of the multifarious circumstances of fellow human beings.

A most important and brilliant ruling issued by the Tzfat Rabbinical Court in 2014 concerning a *get* (bill of divorce) by which a woman was freed of her status as an *aguna* — a woman who cannot get remarried — was suddenly challenged by the Supreme Rabbinical Court of Israel who sought to nullify the *get*.[3] The latter completely ignored the fact that such a move is not only halachically intolerable,[4] but undermines the very institution of Jewish divorce itself. I could offer many more such examples.

How can it be that such things are carried out or even expressed in the name of Judaism and Jewish Law? Anyone who has the

---

2. Rabbi Aharon Lichtenstein, the late foremost leader of Modern Orthodoxy and *Rosh ha-Yeshiva* of Yeshivat Har Etzion, condemned this atrocity in the strongest terms: "A person, whatever his former merits may have been, departed this world while engaged in perpetrating an act of awful and terrible slaughter, *tevach ayom ve-nora*, and thereby, beyond the crime itself, desecrated the name of Heaven, trampled upon the honor of the Torah and *mitzvot*, soiled and sullied the image of *Kenesset Yisrael*, and endangered the future of [Jewish] settlement in Judea, Samaria, and Gaza..." See Rabbi Aharon Lichtenstein's letter in "A Rabbinic Exchange on Baruch Goldstein's Funeral," *Tradition* 28, no. 4 (1994): 59.

3. The case involved a woman whose husband, injured in a motorcycle accident, had been in a persistent vegetative state for seven years. The Tzfat court decided to give her a *get ziku'i* — a divorce document issued on behalf of the husband. See "Heter Aguna she-Ba'ala Tzemach be-Emtza'ut Ziku'i Get," Bet ha-Din ha-Rabbani 861974/2. Documentation regarding this case can be accessed at: http://www.dintora.org/article/195/; http://www.daat.ac.il/daat/psk/psk.asp?id=1054; http://www.daat.ac.il/daat/psk/psk.asp?id=1069; http://www.daat.ac.il/daat/psk/psk.asp?id=1082. For a discussion of this case, see Michael J. Broyde, "Plonit v. Ploni: The Get from the Man in a Permanent Vegetative State," *Hakirah* 18 (Winter 2014): 59–90.

4. See *Mordechai, Hilchot Gittin*, section 455, quoting *Rabbenu Tam*.

slightest knowledge of Judaism is fully aware that nothing within genuine Jewish Law would condone or even suggest such outlandish ideas and immoral acts as those mentioned above.

How does this happen?

Pan-Halacha

Throughout the years, several rabbinical authorities have made the major and dangerous mistake of reducing Judaism to a matter of law alone, a kind of Pan-Halacha (a phrase coined by Heschel). They sincerely believe that Judaism consists only of rigid rules. In this way, they are paradoxically similar to Spinoza, who was also of this opinion and therefore rejected his faith. He referred to it as obsessive, a type of behaviorism, and an extreme form of legalism.[5] That Spinoza made this claim is one thing, but the fact that these learned rabbis now appear to agree with him is an unforgivable blunder. Nothing is further from the truth than to label Judaism as a legal religious system without spirit, poetry, and musical resonance. This is proven by the vast religious Jewish literature that deals with non-halachic matters.

The main reason for this terrible mistake is that these rabbis have failed to study the basic moral values of Judaism as they appear in the book of *Bereshit*. It is well known that, with a few exceptions, this book does not contain laws; it is mainly narrative. To appreciate this, one needs to consider the following.

In this first biblical book, we encounter Avraham and Sara, Yitzhak and Rivka, Yaakov, Rachel and Leah as the primary actors. They are considered the first Jews in history. But how could they have been Jews if the Torah was given only hundreds of years later to Moshe at Mount Sinai? Although a Jew is a Jew even if they do

---

5. See, for example, Benedict de Spinoza, *A Theologico-Political Treatise*, chaps. 3, 4, 13, in *The Chief Works of Benedict de Spinoza*, trans. R.H.M. Elwes (London: G. Bell and Sons, 1883), vol. 1.

not observe the laws of the Torah, it is still the Torah that defines them as such. How, then, could the *Avot* and *Imahot* (Patriarchs and Matriarchs) be full-fledged Jews when the Torah was denied to them? Would it not have been logical to have given the Torah to them long before Moshe? Only upon receiving the Torah could they have been real Jews! So why was it withheld from them?[6]

The answer is crucial. No law, including divine law, can function if it is not preceded by a narrative of the human moral condition and the introduction of basic ethical and religious values. These values cannot be *given*; they must develop *within*, through life experiences. No academic instruction, not even when given by God, would be of any benefit. Such ethics need to develop gradually, on an existential level, and be predicated on innate values that God grants to each person at the moment he or she is born; a kind of categorical imperative in the human soul.

More than that, laws become impersonal, and even dangerous, if they cannot deal with emotions and the enormous moral paradoxes encountered by human beings. As a result, they run the risk of becoming inhuman and even cruel.

It is for that reason that God did not give the laws of the Torah to the *Avot*. First there was a need to learn through personal trials and tribulations. The *Avot* and *Imahot* had to see with their own eyes what happens when people are not governed by law. But most important, they had to become aware of basic moral values, such as the fact that all human beings are created in the image of God, that all are equal, that human life is holy, and that there is only one God Who is at the root of all morality. Only after people have been deeply affected by these ideas and values can law be introduced as a way to put it all into action.

---

6. See *Mishna Kiddushin* 4:14, where the sages state that Avraham observed the commandments. *Bereshit Rabba*, Vilna ed., 79:6 states that Yaakov kept Shabbat; Ibid., 92:4 states that Yosef kept Shabbat. For a discussion on the topic of whether the *Avot* were considered Jews or Noahides, see *Talmudic Encyclopedia*, s.v. "Avot (ha-uma)," 1:36–37.

It was only after the existential and moral turmoil in which the Patriarchs and Matriarchs frequently found themselves, as well as their often problematic encounters with God, that a true religious awareness was born. This consciousness continued to work its way, with all its ups and downs, through the bondage in Egypt, the Exodus, and the splitting of the Reed Sea. Not until that point was there a chance that the law could be received on Mount Sinai, and be beneficial. And even then it was not entirely successful, as seen in the many disturbing biblical stories about the Israelites failing to live up to the law in Moshe's days and long afterward.

But it is not just the fact that narrative, ethical values, and the encounter with the Divine are necessary to have before the law can be given. There is another important message: no law, including divine, can function without constantly and continually taking guidance from these preceding values. There is almost nothing worse than divine law operating on its own, without primary, innate moral values. It runs the risk of turning wild and causing great harm. It needs to be constrained.

This is the purpose of *Sefer Bereshit*.[7] It is a biting critique of the halachic system when Halacha is applied without acknowledging that these prior moral values are needed in order for it to function. *The book of Bereshit*, then, *keeps Halacha under control. It restricts and regulates it, and ensures that it will not wreak havoc.*

Truly great *poskim* (Legal decision makers), cannot lay down their decisions on the basis of Jewish Law alone. The *Shulchan Aruch* (Code of Jewish Law) of Rabbi Yosef Karo and the *Mishne Torah* of Rambam can become dangerous if applied in a vacuum. What *poskim* must realize is that they need to incorporate the great religious and moral values for which *Sefer Bereshit* stands.

---

7. See R. Naftali Zvi Yehuda Berlin (Netziv), *Ha'emek Davar*, introduction to *Bereshit*.

Chosenness

The foremost point of departure in any halachic decision must be that all people are created in the image of God and that all human life is holy. While different tasks, inclinations, and historical events should be recognized and considered when making distinctions between people, no discrimination can ever be tolerated. Halacha should surely acknowledge that the Jews are different from other nations, but only as long as it recognizes that other nations can make contributions that Jews cannot.[8]

For Jews to be the Chosen People, they need to recognize that this in no way can ever mean that they may look down on others. What it *does* mean is that they have an obligation to inspire the world, as a teacher inspires a student even while recognizing that the student may be more gifted than the teacher.

It cannot be denied that throughout our long history this may have been forgotten and laws have appeared that have not always lived up to these standards. Even biblical laws seem to have violated this principle. On several occasions they demanded that Jews show no mercy for some Gentile nations living near or in the Land of Israel in biblical times.[9] But a closer look makes it clear that these laws were contrary to the original divine plan and reveal a kind of divine concession to highly unfortunate circumstances.[10] The laws in question were meant to deal with these nations' ongoing violence and immorality, which had to be dealt with so that Jews could survive and uphold moral standards for the good of all humanity.[11]

---

8. *Ohr ha-Chaim* on *Shemot* 18:21, toward the end. See also Nathan Lopes Cardozo, "Moshe's Fatigue and the Need for a Gentile's Advice" (Thoughts to Ponder 284), *David Cardozo Academy*, Feb. 9, 2012, https://www.cardozoacademy.org/thoughts-to-ponder/moshes-fatigue-and-the-need-for-a-gentiles-advice-ttp-284/.

9. *Devarim* 7:1–2.

10. See *Jewish Law as Rebellion: A Plea for Religious Authenticity and Halachic Courage*, chap. 27, where I explain this concept at length.

11. Many rabbinical laws were instituted for similar reasons. They were mainly introduced as protective measures to ensure that Jews would not suffer at the hands of anti-Semites.

Never should chosenness mean an aloofness or disinterest in the spiritual welfare of non-Jews.[12] *All rulings that oppose this fact are as anti-halachic as they can be,* violating the very cornerstones of Judaism and based on reckless ideas endorsed by those who invent them on their own and then promote them as Halacha without the backing of any authentic, traditional halachic source. They should be condemned and denounced using all means available to us.

Anti-Halacha and Amalek

Highly disturbing is the case concerning Israel's arch-enemy, the Amalekites, the Nazis of biblical times. Divine law required

---

At other times, laws were introduced to counter assimilation and undesirable non-Jewish influences. While these laws seem to discriminate against Gentiles, in truth they were meant to protest against those Gentiles who had low moral standards or were committed criminals and were nearly as evil as the Nazis in later days. These laws did not pertain to civilized non-Jews. See the many observations of the great Talmudic commentator Menachem ha-Me'iri (1249-1316) in *Bet ha-Bechira*—for example, his commentary on *Sanhedrin* 57a and *Avoda Zara* 2a. Surely these laws should be abolished because they run contrary to the principle of divine equality as taught by the Torah. Perhaps any law that gives the impression that non-Jews are discriminated against, such as the law that non-Jews are allowed to do some work for Jews on Shabbat (the "Shabbos goy"), should be abolished, unless Jews will do certain work for Gentiles that they can't do on Sunday and their festivals. The fact that the State of Israel is still dependent on the "Shabbos goy" is highly problematic and inconsistent with the principle of national independence. Daring and innovative rabbinical decisions are far overdue. Violating Shabbat to save the lives of Jews and non-Jews is an absolute obligation. There is no doubt that Avraham, Yitzhak, and Yaakov would have done so. See Netziv's introduction to *Bereshit* in his *Ha'emek Davar*

12. See R. Yisrael Lipschitz (1782–1860) in his commentary *Tiferet Yisrael* on *Avot* 3:14. Rabbi Lipschitz states that the following Gentiles were pious and will enjoy a share in the World to Come: (1) Edward Jenner (1749–1823), who discovered the vaccine against smallpox; (2) Sir Francis Drake (c. 1540–1596), who (according to Rabbi Lipschitz) brought the potato to Europe, thereby saving many people from starvation; (3) Johannes Gutenberg (c. 1398–1468), the inventor of the movable printing press; and (4) Johannes Reuchlin (1455–1522), who was a great friend of the Jews and put his life on the line in order to prevent the burning of the Talmud under the decree issued by the Viennese Emperor Maximilian in the year 1502. See Chaim Rapoport, *The Messiah Problem: Berger, the Angel, and the Scandal of Reckless Indiscrimination* (Ilford UK: Ilford Synagogue, 2002), 88. See also the beautiful observations about Gentiles by Chief Rabbi Avraham Yitzhak ha-Kohen Kook (1865–1935), the famous Talmudist, halachic authority, and kabbalist, in *Igrot ha-Rayah* (Jerusalem: Mossad HaRav Kook, 2006), 142 (letter no. 112).

the Jews to wipe this nation off the face of the earth, including women and children. Such a law runs contrary to our innate moral intuition and the very values promulgated by *Sefer Bereshit*. Commentators have therefore gone overboard to explain this law in different ways, since they were unable to accept that such a commandment could ever have come from God Himself. Some even believed that God tested the Jews to see whether they would understand their calling and thus refuse to implement this genocide,[13] similar to the way that Avraham refused to listen to God in the case of Sedom and Amora when he uttered the famous words: "Shall the whole world's Judge not act justly?"[14] The commentators' attempt is not apologetic, but rather the outcome of their absolute conviction, based on Sefer Bereshit, that there could be no other explanation. At a later stage, they decided that the nation of Amalek no longer existed and that they could abolish the whole law.[15]

It is remarkable that the sages seem to have reacted similarly in the case of other biblical laws, such as that of the *ir ha-nidachat*, in which the commandment is to annihilate the entire Jewish population in a city rampant with idolatry and immorality. The law was declared inoperative from the very start.[16] Another example is the case of the *ben sorer u-moreh*, the rebellious son who had to be executed. Here, too, the law was declared defective and only

---

13. See *Yoma* 22b where King Shaul, who was commanded to kill the Amalekites (2 *Shmuel*, chap. 15), exclaimed: "If the adults have sinned, what is the sin of the children?" According to one problematic source (*Yoma* 22b), God responded that he should not be overly righteous. But in *Midrash Tanchuma*, Buber ed., *Tzav* 5, God "changed His mind" after Moshe showed Him the injustice of the commandment (*Devarim* 20:16–17) to wipe out the women and children of the seven nations.

14. *Bereshit* 18:25.

15. *Mishna Yadayim* 4:4; *Berachot* 28a. There is even a tradition that the fulfillment of this commandment is deferred until the messianic age. See *Radbaz* on *Mishne Torah*, *Hilchot Melachim* 5:5.

16. *Devarim* 13: 13–19; *Sanhedrin* 71a.

seen as a way to teach some important moral lessons.[17] In other instances, the sages seem to have been of the opinion that laws such as those regarding the *mamzer* (a child from an incestuous relationship) and *agunot*[18] should be severely limited to make them almost inoperative, and they often looked for loopholes to find a way out.[19] While it remains a question why they did not completely revoke these laws, it seems clear that in all of these cases it was the overriding moral principles of *Sefer Bereshit* that motivated them.[20]

The sages struggled, reinterpreted, and sometimes even abolished these laws because they fully understood that without the moral religious values developed in *Sefer Bereshit*, halachic chaos would reign and grave injustices would be done.

It is for this reason that some of the greatest tragedies of Judaism in modern times are caused by the fact that some halachic authorities, as well as people like Yigal Amir and Baruch Goldstein, forgot to study the first book of the Torah. They became so dedicated to the letter of the law and to misplaced religious fervor that they did the inconceivable and caused the degradation of Halacha.

It is time for the rabbinic community to make it abundantly clear that no Halacha can ever be implemented without it resting firmly on the values of *Sefer Bereshit*. Only in that way will a healthy Halacha be guaranteed, and severe damage, evil, and the profanation of God's name prevented.

Throughout the thousands of years of our history, Israel's sages and religious leaders — unlike those of the Christians and

---

17. *Devarim* 21:18–21; *Sanhedrin* 71a.
18. For a notable example of a rabbinical attempt to free the wives of missing soldiers from their *aguna* status, see R. Ovadia Yosef, *Yabia Omer*, vol. 6, *Even ha-Ezer*, no. 3.
19. For a full discussion see my book, *Jewish Law as Rebellion*, chapter 27.
20. For a discussion, see Eliezer Berkovits, *Ha-Halacha, Kocha ve-Tafkida* (Jerusalem: Mossad HaRav Kook, 1981).

Muslims — never called on their fellow Jews to wage religious wars against the Gentile world. To them, this was a repulsive idea. At the most, they asked the Almighty to deal with their enemies. This matter stands out in all of Israel's history. Let us be proud of that and not change the rules of the game, unless it is a matter of unequivocal self-defense.

Questions to Ponder
from the DCA Think Tank

1. Do you think that the statement that "more and more of the unacceptable is being done and said in its [Halacha's] name" historically accurate? Or do you think that this has always been the case? After all, we have always had the concept of *Naval Birshut HaTorah* — that an individual is able to act inappropriately by going according to the rules written in the Torah. If this trend is on the rise why do you think this might be?

2. Rabbi Cardozo argues that the richness and moral qualities of the narrative in Bereshit is intended to balance out Halacha. From your reading the stories within the Sefer, do you think that a clear moral voice emerges based on the actions of the Patriarchs and Matriarchs?

3. Rabbi Cardozo writes that "Throughout the thousands of years of our history, Israel's sages and religious leaders — unlike those of the Christians and Muslims — never called on their fellow Jews to wage religious wars against the Gentile world. To them, this was a repulsive idea." To what extent do you think this is due to an inherent tendency in

Judaism to condemn violence as opposed to the fact that Jews generally didn't possess the political power that would have made that option possible? Could it be that the re-establishment of the State of Israel reawakened a genie that was always present, but dormant, within Judaism?

Bereshit

The Unknowable, Loving, and Aggravating God

בראשית ברא אלוהים את השמים ואת הארץ

In the beginning God created the
heaven and the earth. *Bereshit 1:1*

The riddles of God are more satisfying than
the solutions of man. –*G.K. Chesterton*[1]

JEWISH TRADITION FORBIDS the pronunciation of the four-letter name of God. This name, rooted in the Hebrew word for "being," consists of the Hebrew letters: Yud, Heh, Vav, and Heh. According to the Sages, the name reflects the various dimensions of "being" related to time: past, present and future. As such, God figures as the One Who lives in these three dimensions and exists *simultaneously* in all three. This actually makes these dimensions all one, which means that God is completely beyond time, while paradoxically existing also within the confines of time. And that is why human beings are not allowed to pronounce this name, for if they were to do so, they would give the impression that they actually understand the unfathomable concept that God

---

1. G.K.C. as M.C.; *Being a Collection of Thirty-Seven Introductions by G.K. Chesterton*, selected and edited by J.P. de Fonseka, "Introduction to the Book of Job," (London: Methuen & Co. Ltd., 1929), 47.

lives simultaneously in the past, present, future, and beyond.[2] That would be an untruth, and Jewish law forbids lying. God is incomprehensible and beyond all description.[3] He can only be *addressed*; His being cannot be *expressed*.[4]

The great Kabbalist Rabbi Moshe Cordovero (1522-1570) elaborates on this in his famous work *Elima Rabati*:

> When your intellect conceives of God...do not permit yourself to imagine that there is a God as depicted by you. For if you do this, you will have a finite and corporeal conception of God, God forbid. Instead, your mind should dwell only on the affirmation of God's existence, *and then it should recoil*. To do more than this is to allow the imagination to reflect upon God as He is in Himself and such reflection is bound to result in imaginative limitations and corporeality. Therefore, put reins on your intellect and do not allow it too great a freedom, but assert God's existence and deny your intellect the possibility of comprehending Him. The mind should run to and fro — running to affirm God's existence and recoiling from any limitations, since man's imagination pursues his intellect.[5]

A THREE-DIMENSIONAL REALITY ON A FLAT SURFACE

Introducing God is one of the most difficult things to do. It is like presenting a three-dimensional reality on a flat surface. Still, God is the most captivating figure in human history and His track

---

2. The only person who was allowed to pronounce God's full name was the High Priest on Yom Kippur in the Holy of Holies, the single place where time did not seem to play a role. (See *Yoma* 39b; *Kiddushin* 71a).

3. See *Yoma* 69b; Rabbi E.E. Dessler, *Michtav Me-Eliyahu* (Yerushalayim: The Committee for the Publication of the Writings of Rabbi E.E. Dessler, 1987), 3:315.

4. Donald J. Moore, *Martin Buber: Prophet of Religious Secularism* (Fordham University Press, 1996), 134.

5. *Elima Rabati* (Lvov, 1881) 1:10, p. 4b, translated by Louis Jacobs in *Principles of the Jewish Faith: An Analytical Study* (Eugene, OR: Wipf & Stock, 2009), 125.

record is most unusual. His deeds are unprecedented, yet very disturbing. He is to be loved, but often irritates. He transcends human limitation, but He gets angry and downright emotional. He is beyond criticism, yet He is judged by the strictest criteria of justice. Religious people believe that He is the only One Who really has it all together and knows what He is doing. But others are convinced that He is absent-minded, allows matters to get out of hand, and causes unnecessary pain to some of His creations.

Nobody has ever been the cause of so much controversy, deafening silence, and admiration. And no one is so conspicuous, even while using an ingenious hideout, which we call the universe. Though He is the great mystery in our lives, some people have a relationship with Him as if He were their best friend, one with Whom they can converse and to Whom they can complain. He is the personal psychologist of millions, but is ultimately blamed for anything that goes wrong. Others deny His existence because of the many inconsistencies in His behavior. And then there are those who believe in Him but, out of anger or frustration, refuse to speak to Him. In the words of famous novelist and poet Miguel de Cervantes, "Man appoints, and God disappoints."[6]

Who is this strange figure called God?

It's important to realize that the term, "God" is used arbitrarily. It often stands for completely opposing entities used by religious and quasi-religious ideologies. All of them agree that "God" affirms some absolute reality as the ultimate. But they fundamentally disagree as to what that reality entails. For Benedict Spinoza, the Dutch philosopher and supreme Jewish rebel, as for other pantheistic thinkers, He is really an "It," a primal, impersonal force, identical with nature — some ineffable, immutable, impassive Divine substance that pervades the universe, or *is* the universe.

---

6. Miguel de Cervantes, *The History of the Ingenious Gentleman, Don Quixote of La Mancha*, trans. from Spanish by Peter Anthony Motteux (London: Hurst, Robinson, and Co., 1822), 5:137.

God is only immanent, not transcendent; a Divine spirit that has little practical meaning in a person's day-to-day life.

Although this view is close to the kabbalistic idea of *Ein Sof* (the Endless and Boundless One), this is not identical to the Jewish perception of God. In the Jewish tradition, God is not just an idea or a blind force. God is the *Ribono shel Olam*, the Master of the Universe, Who is both immanent and transcendent, surpassing the universe, which is His creation. He has the disturbing habit of being everywhere and anywhere, and He is known to interfere with anything and everything. He is a living God, a dynamic power in the life and history of humanity, moving things around when He sees fit, smiling when He is pleased with the behavior of His creatures and annoyed when they have blundered yet again. But most important, while He does not fit into any category, He has — for lack of a better word — "personality," and His own consciousness. Indeed, His essence cannot be expressed, but He can definitely be addressed.

THE OBSESSIVE FASCINATION WITH HALACHA AS A SUBSTITUTE

No doubt this is the reason why religious Jews spend little time *discussing* God, to the extent that it can seem as if they have expelled Him from their emotional and intellectual lives. This may explain their "obsessive" fascination with Halacha, God's Law; it offers the only way to draw close to Him. Their intense preoccupation with Halacha compensates for their inability to discuss His very Being, as Prof. Haym Soloveitchik writes:

> Zealous to continue traditional Judaism unimpaired, religious Jews seek to ground their new emerging spirituality less on a now unattainable intimacy with Him, than on an intimacy with His Will, avidly eliciting Its intricate demands and saturating their daily lives with Its exactions. Having

lost the touch of His presence, they seek now solace in the pressure of His yoke.⁷

This, however, has led to great problems in Jewish education, because it has ignored the enormous need of searching young people to actually discuss basic issues concerning faith, theology, and the meaning of life, on which the whole premise of Halacha stands or falls. Even prayer, which is the most direct way to address God, has by now been so "halachized" that in many synagogues it is the *laws* concerning prayer that have taken precedence, often at the expense of realizing to Whom one is actually speaking! It was the Hassidic Movement — with its emphasis on the actual *experience* of prayer — that tried to respond to this acute problem. It is not surprising that this has led to some antinomian tendencies within the Hassidic movement.⁸

The radical differences in the conception of God make for an equally profound divergence in attitudes about all of life and the universe. While in pantheistic and other non-monotheistic philosophies, God has no moral input, nothing could be further from the Jewish concept of God. In Judaism, He is the source par excellence of all moral criteria, although He *seems* to violate some moral standards in the way He deals with people. Apparently, this is due to the fact that He needs to achieve certain goals with His creation that are known only to Him, and remain unintelligible to humans. God's perfection, then, is not that He is already perfect but that He strives for it. If He were to be perfect, He would lack the capacity to *become* perfect, which would be a terrible deficiency in His being.⁹

---

7. Haym Soloveitchik, "Rupture and Reconstruction: The Transformation of Contemporary Orthodoxy," *Tradition* 28, no. 4 (1994): 103.
8. See Shaul Magid, *Hasidism on the Margin: Reconciliation, Antinomianism, and Messianism in Izbica-Radzin Hasidism*, (Madison, WI: The University of Wisconsin Press, 2003).
9. One is reminded of American writer and philosopher Elbert Hubbard's famous observation: "Life is a paradox. Every truth has its counterpart which contradicts it; and every

Pantheism

According to pantheism, the world is eternal, with no beginning. As such, it has no intrinsic purpose, since purpose is the conscious motivation of a creator to bring something into existence. It therefore follows that in the pantheistic view, human beings, too, have no ultimate purpose. They, like the universe, just *are*. Moral behavior may have some utilitarian purpose, but no ultimate one. For radical pantheists, acting morally is not the goal of humans; it is simply a means to their survival, a way to prevent pain and achieve happiness.

On a deeper level, some pantheists view the universe as an illusion — a flux of sensory deception — to be escaped. Made from a purely Divine substance, it cannot accommodate any physical reality and therefore can have no real meaning. In that case, neither can humans. Once their physical existence is branded an illusion, they can no longer be of flesh and blood. Nor are their deeds of any real value. Since it is the body that enables people to act, and the body is part of the deception, it must follow that all human behavior belongs to the world of illusion.

It is this view that Judaism protests against. God is a conscious Being, Who created the world with a purpose. This world is real and by no means a mirage. People's deeds are of great value, far from an illusion. While they may not be the primary goal of creation,[10] they are of enormous importance. Judaism objects to the pantheistic view of human beings, which depersonalizes them, and must ultimately lead to their demoralization. If people are part of an illusion, so are their feelings. Why, then, be concerned with a fellow human's emotional and physical welfare?

---

philosopher supplies the logic for his own undoing." *Selected writings of Elbert Hubbard* (New York: W. H. Wise & co., 1922), 9:408.

10. See below "The Idolatry of Theodicy" on page 57

Paradoxically, this version of pantheism infiltrated Western culture via the back door. When we are told by certain modern philosophers that a person is "merely" physical, and that the body is "merely" a mechanical mechanism in which emotions are just a chemical inconvenience, we are confronted with pantheism turned on its head. While pantheism denies the physical side of existence, this scientific approach rejects the *spiritual* dimension of a human being. In both cases, emotions are seen as part of an illusion, and therefore of lesser importance.

God's Emotions

Judaism, on the other hand, declares that emotions are what make the person; they are real and of crucial importance. In fact, emotions are central to human existence, since they are the foundation of moral behavior. It is for this reason that Judaism views God as an emotional Being. Metaphorically attributing emotions to God raises emotions to a supreme level. If God has emotions such as love, mercy, jealousy, and anger, then these feelings must be genuine, important, and not to be taken lightly in humans.

While some philosophers considered such anthropomorphism scandalous, the Jewish tradition took the risk of granting God emotions so as to uphold morality on its highest level and guarantee that it would not be tampered with. For the sake of humans, even God is prepared to compromise His complete Otherness, albeit not to the point where He would be regarded as a human being.

In Western society, God has become insignificant. While the vast majority of people declare their belief in God, they seem to add two words to their declaration of faith: "I believe in God; *so what?*" In this way, the most radical encounter a person could ever have with the Master of the Universe is reduced to a senseless blur of charlatanism. It is to this that Judaism objects. Abraham Joshua

Heschel put it very plainly: "God is of no importance unless He is of supreme importance."[11]

Or is He?

Questions to Ponder
from the DCA Think Tank

1. "Instead your mind should openly dwell on the affirmation of God's existence and then it should recoil." Does Jewish prayer, as currently or previously prescribed, fit with this admonition by Rabbi Moshe Cordovero? Could we, or should we, take something from this sentiment to transform our prayer experience?

2. Does it trouble you that God doesn't adhere to the "moral" standards He has set for humankind? In general, does it bother you that you don't understand the ways of God? Have you ever wished He had created us with the ability to decipher His ways (at least to some degree), or been angry that this is not the case?

3. As mentioned by Rabbi Cardozo, Dr. Haym Soloveitchik in his seminal article "Rupture and Reconstruction" discusses the focus in contemporary modern Orthodoxy on learning Halacha through text (as opposed to experientially) as follows:

   > Zealous to continue traditional Judaism unimpaired, religious Jews seek to ground their new emerging spirituality less on a now unattainable intimacy with Him, than on an

---

11. Abraham Joshua Heschel, *God in Search of Man: A Philosophy of Judaism* (NY: Farrar, Straus and Giroux, 1955), 153.

intimacy with His Will, avidly eliciting Its intricate demands and saturating their daily lives with Its exactions. Having lost the touch of His presence, they now seek solace in the pressure of His yoke.

    a. Do you feel that spirituality can still emerge, notwithstanding a shift from intimacy with God to intimacy with His will?

    b. Aside from these explanations, can you think of other reasons for the lack of "God talk" in some halachic circles today? Could "God" simply be an emotionally-laden topic, making people who are "less emotional types" (more rational/practical) uncomfortable—and hence the more rationalistic-leaning modern Orthodox community largely avoids it…?

4. "In fact, emotions are central to human existence, since they are the foundation of moral behavior. It is for this reason that Judaism views God as an emotional Being." Do you view God as an emotional Being? Why or why not? Do you agree that emotion is the foundation of moral behavior?

5. If emotion is indeed the foundation of both the ability to discuss/experience God, and of moral behavior, then should not the "less emotional types" we mentioned in question 3 above be encouraged to learn to connect better with their own emotions (overcome blocks and inhibitions and open their hearts to vulnerability)? After all, as Rabbi Cardozo points out, this issue has ramifications for young people, the synagogue space, and much more, and as such, is potentially very damaging.

The Lessons of Religious Optimism

זה ספר תולדת אדם ביום ברא אלהים אדם
בדמות אלהים עשה אתו זכר ונקבה בראם ויברך
אתם ויקרא את שמם אדם ביום הבראם

These are the records of Adam's generations. When God created man, He made him in the likeness of God; male and female He created them. And when they were created, He blessed them and called them Adam. *Bereshit 5:1-2*

JEWISH TRADITION HAS never denied that God is the creator of evil. The Bible itself attests to this: "I make peace and create evil."[1] The sages never lived in a psychological vacuum denying the realities of life. There was no attempt to cover up all the terrible things that could befall man. They tried only to understand where evil belonged in the scheme of the divine creation.

All religions and philosophies are confronted with the question of how to relate to "existence." Should one oppose "existence" and ideally opt for "non-existence," or should one view "being" as good and "non-being" as the opposite?

The great rabbinical schools of Beit Shammai and Beit Hillel confronted exactly this question. In a most unusual debate, which

---

1. Yeshayahu 45:7.

lasted two and a half years, they discussed whether it is better for humans to have been created or not to have been created.² Their conclusion is startling: It is better for humans *not* to have been created; but now that they *have* been created, let them examine their deeds. This would seem to be a very pessimistic view! But is it really?

Arthur Schopenhauer, a prominent nineteenth-century German philosopher and author of *The World as Will and Idea*, could perhaps be regarded as Europe's greatest pessimist. In his works, Schopenhauer has not one good word to say in favor of "existence." From his younger days, he viewed the world as an ongoing disaster and lived in constant fear that things would only deteriorate. Danger is rampant, so he decides to sleep with a weapon under his pillow and refuses to have the barber shave him with a knife, lest he cut his throat. The only one he has faith in is his dog; as for Man, there is no one to trust. Life is an ongoing deceit, harsh and cruel.

How is it, then, that some people live joyfully and see everything in a sanguine light? Why are there optimists in this world, who deny the truth and ignore the fact that this life is really a catastrophe? Can they not see reality?

Well, argues Schopenhauer, the aggressively optimistic philosophers of the Western world have fallen prey to vulgar buoyancy that is rooted in the Jewish tradition! Jewish traditional optimism reflects a "self-congratulatory human egoism, which is blind to all except our [own] all too frail human goals and aspirations."³

Yes, believe it or not, Jews are guilty of bringing some optimism into the world.

Is it indeed true that Judaism is blind to the tragic? Nobody can deny that Judaism adopts an optimistic view of life, but is

---

2. Eruvin 13b.
3. *Works*, R.B. Haldane and J. Kemp trans., London, Kegan Paul, Trench: Trubner and Co., 1909, vol. III, pp. 305ff, 446ff

this optimism vulgar and self-destructive, and are we unable, as a result of this shortsightedness, to cope in the face of disaster?

> Rabbi Shimon said: "In the hour that God was about to create Adam, the angels of service were divided. Some said, 'Let him not be created.' Others said, 'Let him be created.' Love said, 'Let him be created, for he will do loving deeds.' But Truth said, 'Let him not be created, for he will be all falsity.' Righteousness said, 'Let him be created, for he will do righteous deeds.' Peace said, 'Let him not be created, because he will be full of strife.' What did the Holy One Blessed be He do? He seized hold of Truth and cast it to the earth [where it broke into pieces], as it says: 'You cast truth to the ground.' (Daniel 8:12)"[4]

Virtually no midrash should be taken *literally*. Every midrash, however, should be taken *seriously*. When midrashim speak about the origin of mankind, they are trying to give us insight into the human condition. No doubt this is the case with this midrash as well. It is, however, clearly disturbing, because it makes the point that truth needs to be "thrown to the ground" before we could be created. It appears that not even God can create human beings unless a compromise is made in which truth pays the price. There is no "all is well" attitude when mankind comes on the scene. For humans to exist, one has to remove all romantically optimistic views about human existence. Not even the good Lord has the power, so to speak, to indiscriminately silence all opposition. To create humanity is to take a risk, and the pessimists have a point.

Meshech Chochma (Bereshit 1:31) explains that while all creatures were blessed with the pronouncement: "And God saw that it was good," this is not so with mankind. Not even God could "see" (in anthropomorphic terms) what humans would become,

---

4. Bereshit Rabbah 8:5

whether they would be good or bad. God's "seeing," says Meshech Chochma, implies determinism, i.e., that all creatures will follow their unchanging nature.

Only mankind is endowed with free will. He is the great unknown. Hence, the absolute truth, reflected in the existence of God, will have to be compromised, since our very purpose is to be free agents with the ability to deny or ignore God. And so pessimism is born. We may go wrong and indeed we may become a "disaster," as posited by Schopenhauer. The midrash knows that truth is cast to the ground, and all devout Jews know that truth is difficult to bear. But what is the effect of this knowledge? Can it be anything other than despair as Schopenhauer would have it? There is only one possible response. It is as if the midrash has anticipated Schopenhauer: "Then the angels of service said to God, 'Lord of the Universe, how can You despise Your seal [the truth]?' And God responded, 'Let Truth arise from the earth, as it says: Truth springs from the earth.'"[5]

The Jewish concept of *teshuvah* — "returning" — is a protest against Schopenhauer and all dedicated pessimists. To be given the opportunity to do *teshuvah* is an enormous privilege. It is a joy to be able to say I am sorry, to take responsibility for our deeds, to start over. In fact, it is one of the great gifts that Judaism has given mankind: the knowledge that we can change; that if we have not acted rightly, we can turn over a new leaf and start again. This is the ultimate expression of religious optimism. Judaism teaches us that there is no karma that traps us, and no original sin that stands in our way. We are free to re-engage with God and with our fellow man. Whatever obstacles there may be, all that is required is the will to change our ways and the effort to work hard at it.

Certainly, the truth will have to rise from the earth in "broken pieces," but there is a purpose: so that we will labor to rediscover

---

5. Tehillim 85:12

it, fragment by fragment, without ever seeing the full picture. The truth will not be truth for us unless we *discover* it by way of our own effort. Paradoxically, it is our potential to stray that creates a realistic optimism. The Jew clings to life, despite Schopenhauer, because he or she knows that since God was prepared to cast the truth to the ground, there must be a Divine plan beyond mankind's comprehension. That is the foundation of balanced optimism as taught by Jewish tradition.

This, then, is the underlying motive of Judaism. It is a warning not to yield to total pessimism as long as the truth springs from the ground. It is an admonition to endure truth and to choose life. It is a plea to endure, for it is only defiant endurance that reveals the fact that truth, however broken, remains the seal of God.

Questions to Ponder
from the DCA Think Tank

1. The philosopher Schopenhauer had a particular antipathy for Judaism and its worldliness. The truly religious individual, Schopenhauer thought, abhors life and resists the will to live; asceticism is the mark of the true religious life. Do you think that Schopenhauer, without intending it, managed to pay Judaism its deepest compliment? Did he hit on one of Judaism's deepest truths?

2. Contemporary psychologists (e.g. Martin Seligman) speak of the importance of optimism in human flourishing. Pessimism can have a debilitating effect on well-being even though pessimists, so say researchers, often have a more truthful view of themselves than optimists. Then again, there are realistic optimists, who may enjoy the best of both worlds.

Do you agree with Rabbi Cardozo that in the concept of teshuvah (returning) Judaism has succeeded in "bottling" a uniquely powerful formula for affirming life while retaining a truthful sense of one's own shortcomings and fallibility?

3. According to the midrash quoted by Rabbi Cardozo there appear to be two kinds of truth, the heavenly and the earthly. The earthly variety requires effort and we never see the full picture. How do you understand this image of Truth being cast to the earth from where it sprouts anew? Are there kinds of truth which can be acquired only through human effort and experience? If we acknowledge that "we never see the full picture", that at best we see "fragments" of the whole, how does this affect the way we understand the world? How does it affect our approach to political disagreement, for example? How does it affect our approach to personal disagreements and to our personal relationships in general?

4. Rabbi Cardozo speaks of the opportunity to do teshuvah as a "privilege", a "joy", a "gift". The Day of Atonement, Yom Kippur, is the day of the Jewish year given over to the ritual enactment of teshuvah. Its liturgy is replete with expressions of collective self-reproach and self-abasement (the repeated *ashamnu's* and *al heit's* with their accompanying breast-beating) albeit tempered by a unwavering trust in God's desire to forgive. We are not accustomed to think of it as a joyful day. Yet some Hassidic masters cautioned against dwelling too much on negative introspection. Rabbi Yitzhak Meir of Gur argued that excessive reflection on one's sins will pull one down into a state of negativity from which teshuvah will not even be possible. Better to rush through the *"al heit's"* and to focus instead, and joyfully, on the mitzvot one is resolved to do. Which of these versions of Yom Kippur speaks to you? Is joyfulness part of your Yom Kippur emotional palette?

Freud's Subconscious Discovery of God

> ויברא אלהים את האדם בצלמו,
> בצלם אלהים ברא אתו
>
> God created man in His image; in the
> image of God He created him. *Bereshit 1:27*

FREUD HAD NOTHING good to say about religion. He regarded religious beliefs as "...illusions, fulfillments of the oldest, strongest and most urgent wishes of mankind."[1] Religion, he believed, was a mental defense against life's hardships, against its threatening aspects, such as earthquakes, floods, storms, diseases and inevitable death, which "rise up against us, majestic, cruel and inexorable."[2] We look for some kind of security into which we can escape from many of these threatening misfortunes. And if we cannot avoid them, we need to at least feel that these disasters have an exalted purpose. This requires the existence of an ultimate father figure, an infinite being who can stop any disease or natural disaster, or has good reason for causing these calamities to take place.

This, claims Freud, is the reason why millions of people, including highly intelligent ones, believe in God. It is not because they have a high mental capacity to understand this world, but rather

---

1. Sigmund Freud, *The Future of an Illusion*, trans. from the German and ed. by James Strachey, (New York: W.W. Norton & Company, 1961), 30.
2. Ibid. 16.

because of "the universal, obsessive neurosis of humanity,"[3] which would be left behind if people would finally learn to face the world, relying no longer on illusions but upon scientifically authenticated knowledge.

The Oedipus Complex

In *Totem and Taboo*, Freud introduced his famous Oedipus complex.[4] Freud uses this complex to explain the tremendous emotional intensity of religious life and the associated feelings of guilt and obligation to obey the dictates of the deity. He postulates a stage of human pre-history in which the family or tribe unit was the "primal horde," consisting of father, mother and offspring. The father, as head of the family or tribe, retained exclusive rights over all the females and drove away or even killed his sons who challenged his authority. The sons, seeing that they could never challenge their father's authority, decided to kill him and (being cannibals) consume him! This universal complex, says Freud, is the primal crime of which guilt is born, and which is responsible for so much tension within the human psyche.

This guilt ultimately developed into moral inhibitions and other phenomena now found in religion, since the sons, struck with remorse, could not succeed their father as head of the tribe.

For this reason, the father figure — which later developed into the god idea — became so powerful in the human mind, and that is the reason why people are religious: because of a deep feeling of guilt and the need to rectify the killing or rejection of this god by way of total obedience.

Many scholars have discussed and criticized Freud's theory. Clearly, Freud was influenced by Charles Darwin and Robertson

---

3. Ibid. 43.

4. Oedipus is a prominent figure in Greek mythology who unknowingly killed his father and married his mother; the Oedipus complex of Freudian theory is the child's unconscious jealousy of his father and longing for his mother.

Smith, two dominant figures of the 19th century who initiated the "primal horde" theory. Modern anthropologists, such as H.L. Philip in his 1956 publication *Freud and Religious Belief*, have rejected this theory.

While Freud considered himself an atheist and seems to have misunderstood most of religion, he was not entirely wrong when he proposed that many people are religious because they *wish* a God to exist to whom they can turn when in great need. Surprising, however, is his conclusion that *because* we *wish* God to exist, one must conclude that His existence is a fantasy. This makes little sense. The fact that we wish God to exist has no bearing at all on the question of *whether* He really exists or not. He may quite well exist, and we may simultaneously have a great need for His existence.

Nowhere did Freud offer any justification for his atheism, nor did he understand that he had in fact hit on one of the great foundations of Jewish thought.

Jewish tradition teaches that mankind was created in God's image. Whatever this may mean, it definitely includes the fact that God created humans in such a way that they, in desperate need to discover themselves, would constantly search for *Him*. Freud, we believe, gave a most original interpretation of this phenomenon. With his discovery of the father figure, he may have uncovered the mechanism through which God created an idea of Himself as the ultimate Father in the human mind.

Utter dependence

The utter dependence of a child on his or her loving parents may very well have been the way through which God built the foundation for our capacity to believe and trust in Him. One could argue that this was the very reason why God decided in favor of parenthood over other options, such as creating human beings without the need for parents (the creation of Adam and Hava).

Rabbinic tradition suggests that God first created the Torah as a primordial blueprint, after which He created the world accordingly.[5] In that case, He may very well have created the need for us to see Him as the great Father Figure and consequently decided to create the need for parents.[6]

Freud, then, may have been motivated, subconsciously and against his better instincts, by a deep Jewish need to explain the foundation of belief, and in this way he contributed substantially to the great tradition of Torah commentary.

Psychology generally gives us a totally different idea of what we thought we knew best about ourselves. The Jew, Shlomo (Sigmund) Freud, proved this point by believing that his arguments opposed religious faith, while in fact supporting it.

Questions to Ponder
from the DCA Think Tank

1. How do you understand the concept of humans being created in the image of God? That each of us has inherent value? Absolute freedom of will? A creative spark? Consciousness? Discuss.

2. Rather than focusing on guilt, Judaism talks about obligations to keep Mitzvot and discusses the spectrum of carrying out commandments from fear and from love. How do you rank these components in your own religious life? To what extent is guilt a motivating factor in your own observance?

---

5. *Bereshit Rabba*, Vilna ed., 1:1; *Zohar* on *Shemot* 161b.
6. See John H. Hick, *Philosophy of Religion*, 4th Edition (Englewood Cliffs, NJ: Prentice-Hall, 1990), 33-35.

Noah

God and Natural Disasters

> ויאמר אלהים לנח קץ כל בשר בא לפני כי מלאה הארץ חמס מפניהם והנני משחיתם את הארץ
>
> God said to Noah, "I have decided to put an end to all flesh, for the earth is filled with lawlessness because of them: I am about to destroy them with the earth. *Bereshit 6:13*

THROUGHOUT ALL OF human history, mankind has been confronted with enormous and deadly natural disasters. After each disaster, many good souls, Jews and non-Jews, wonder what the higher meaning is behind all this. Religious people, in particular, postulate that there is a divine purpose to these catastrophes, and most of them believe that it must be human moral and religious failure that caused this divine wrath to rain down upon them and their fellow men.

Such reactions and attitudes are part of the outlook on life within religious communities, and there is a strong tendency among some religious people to blame the irreligious for these disasters. Many even blame *themselves* for the lack of their own religiosity and religious observance.

This is especially true of religious Jews. We feel responsible for the shortcomings of mankind and so we endlessly repeat: *mipnei chato'enu*, because of our sins, this has befallen us. Many even believe that disasters visited upon non-Jews are of our making.

While there is something very beautiful about this mindset — not letting us off the hook, even when it is not *we* who are affected, but the gentiles — there is also something very wrong with it. Not only does it play into the hand of anti-Semites, it is also theologically unsound.

It can hardly be denied that the Torah and Jewish tradition are replete with examples of God warning the Jewish people of grave consequences if they do not follow the Divine Will.

Rambam's (Maimonides) famous statement in his *Mishneh Torah* seems to bear this out. The great sage teaches us that after each catastrophe that has befallen the community, Jews should blow trumpets, fast, and repent.[1] To believe that these tragedies are accidental and of no meaning is highly irresponsible, warns Maimonides. It is the epitome of callousness and denial of Divine Providence. It is close to atheism.

Still, this cannot be the whole story. Common sense — and a keen understanding of Jewish religious philosophy and sources — seem to tell us that there is more to this than meets the eye. In fact, the constant emphasis on the moral and religious responsibility of Jews, and mankind at large, for any disaster that befalls them may well be a serious deviation from Jewish religious teachings. While many might argue that any denial of divine retribution would constitute *apikorsut* (heresy), it could very well be that the opposite is heresy and even a form of idol worship.

Is man the measure of all things?

Do good and evil events in this world really always depend on human behavior? Was there no other reason for God to create the universe than to test human beings and reward or punish accordingly? Is man really the measure of all things? Despite the statement quoted above, Rambam seems to doubt this. In his

---
1. Hilchot Ta'anit 1:1-4.

Moreh Nevuchim,[2] he states that God made everything *lema'anehu*,[3] a phrase taken by many commentators to refer to human beings, (i.e. *for the sake of man*), but which Maimonides understands to mean for *His* (i.e. *for God's*) sake rather than for man's.

Are we compelled to believe that black holes and baby universes, the millions of stars and other celestial bodies, were created only to test human moral and religious conduct? Would it not be more logical to conclude that God's reasons for creating the universe are much greater and more significant than the problem of human behavior? Why create planets and invisible baby universes when what is of sole importance is human behavior on one tiny globe? As long as we do not know *why* God created the universe, including so many other worlds, we cannot say for sure whether every calamity is a result of our shortcomings. Some may be, and some may not be.

When Iyov (Job) demands an explanation from God as to why he has lost his children and his wealth, and is suffering such terrible pain, God's response is not that he has in any way misbehaved. Instead, He asks Iyov: "Where were you when I laid the foundations of the earth? Tell me, if you have understanding."[4] God challenges Iyov's very notion that suffering is always related to sin. *Who says that My treatment of human beings is always to be judged by your criteria of righteousness? There are larger issues at work.*

While Iyov's friends argue that he *must* have sinned, God rejects this argument. He declares that such an attitude is a denial of His multidimensional being and His larger cosmic plan. Iyov's suffering has nothing to do with sin. God protests this very idea and tells him it is a declaration of preposterous heresy and an expression of childishness to think that way. Even worse, it is a reflection of

---

2. Part 3, chap. 13.
3. Mishle 16:4
4. *Iyov* 38:4.

human arrogance. Are we really so important? Since when are we able to judge God and decide *why* He created the universe? Such haughtiness is nothing but an attempt to squeeze God into the parameters of what we believe God should be. It is based on preconceived ideas of what God is and is not. We constantly try to view God through our own prism. But that reveals more about us than it does about God. Such an attempt is nothing less than idol worship.

The joy of life

The joy of life, which is so much a part of Jewish tradition, focuses on the fact that from a divine perspective, things could actually be much worse. Despite God's impenetrable nature and thoughts, He shared some of His "good" qualities with us, informing us that our existence has great meaning, though we may never know what that meaning consists of. It is this aspect that is celebrated by Jewish tradition and beckons us to understand that despite all the pain, it is for the most part possible to enjoy life, to attain *simchat chayim*!

The claim that we are responsible for every disaster is an unbearable burden. It is an attitude of hopelessness that may lead us to give up and to see God only as a vengeful God with Whom we cannot have a relationship. It would be better to reason, as does Søren Kierkegaard, that God sometimes applies His "teleological suspension of the ethical"[5] so as to achieve His goals within the universe. This is true not just because we have a philosophical need to see God in terms of his total Otherness, but because it may be closer to the truth. Theodicy, in claiming that God can be justified in *human terms*, is a form of idol worship.

Over the years, Jewish worship has adopted an attitude of

---

5. Søren Kierkegaard, *Fear and Trembling*, eds. C. Stephen Evans and Sylvia Walsh, trans. by Sylvia Walsh (Cambridge: Cambridge University Press, 2006), 46-58.

mipnei chato'enu galinu me'artzenu (because of our sins we have been exiled from our land), which has developed into a form of pessimism that is not loyal to the teachings of our Jewish tradition. It pretends that we are superhuman; this is dangerous and religiously unhealthy.

This approach has infiltrated and dominated too many of our daily prayers, which should be replaced with prayers about God whose exalted greatness is inscrutable, but worthy of our worship.

Humility

Whether or not a devastating fire or any other natural disaster, even if it was started by human beings, is an expression of divine displeasure we do not know. Nor will it ever be known, until we will again be blessed with prophets. Instead, it should evoke in us a feeling of deep humility. It should serve as a wake-up call, that all our boasting, our arrogance, our claiming that we know it all and that one day all of nature will be under our control, is one of the most pathetic dreams humans have ever entertained. One catastrophic storm can bring all of the world's population to its knees.

No doubt we should treat each disaster *as if* it were a warning, a call for repentance, for humility, and even more a call to help wherever we can. The dangerous apathy of many of us in the wake of such terrible tragedy is perhaps the most devastating expression of human failure.

We must be fully aware that calamities are perhaps part of God's cosmic plan far beyond human behavior, and we are not to be blamed. This is an important message to send to our young people, lest they despair under the yoke of religious pessimism. Better a God Who is incomprehensible than a God Who unremittingly causes us to feel that all catastrophes are our fault. Believing the latter is un-Jewish.

More will be said on this in the next chapter.

Questions to Ponder
from the DCA Think Tank

1. Do you agree with Rabbi Cardozo's claim that the rationale of *"mipnei chato'enu"*—because of human sin, we have been exiled—is dangerous and unhealthy, pretending as it does that man is superhuman? If so, do you think guilt is ever a productive motivating force? If not, what do you think can protect those who do adopt this approach from the concerns Rabbi Cardozo expresses?

2. In the *Mishneh Torah*, Rambam prescribes fasting and repentance when bad things happen in the world, indicating a belief that those bad events are not random, but the will of God—as is everything that happens in the world. But in *Moreh Nevuchim*, Rambam suggests that God created the world for Himself, implying that the tests to man's faith are immaterial. How do you reconcile these two approaches of Rambam?

3. If it is not mankind's business to know why good and bad things happen in this world (as God informs Job), how do you assimilate the explicit biblical message that "reward" and "punishment" are directly caused by good or bad actions (seen, for example, in the second paragraph of the Shema)? And doesn't this idea also undermine the force of God's instruction to us that we should do good—for if not, bad will befall us?

4. Given the conclusion of Bet Shammai and Bet Hillel that man would have been better off not having been created, what gets you out of bed in the morning?

The Idolatry of Theodicy

> ויאמר ה' לנח בא אתה וכל ביתך אל התבה
> כי אתך ראיתי צדיק לפני בדור הזה
>
> Then the Eternal said to Noah, "Go into the ark, with all your household, for you alone have I found righteous before Me in this generation. *Bereshit 7:1*

> I believe that if a triangle could speak, it would say...that God is eminently triangular, while a circle would say that the divine nature is eminently circular. Thus each would ascribe to God its own attributes, would assume itself to be like God and look on everything else as ill-shaped. — *Baruch Spinoza*[1]

IN THE LAST chapter, I suggested that from an authentic Jewish point of view, it is a mistake to hold humankind or the Jewish people morally responsible for natural disasters such as earthquakes, tsunamis, hurricanes, or fires. Though *some* disasters may indeed be due to our failures, it is in fact irresponsible and dangerous to make human beings responsible for every disaster;

---

1. Benedict de Spinoza, Letter 60 (56) "Between Spinoza and Hugo Boxel on Ghosts," in *Improvement of the Understanding, Ethics and Correspondence*, trans. R.H.M. Elwes (New York: Cosimo, 2006), 392.

it reflects the same mistake the friends of the biblical Iyov (Job) made when they assumed that he must have sinned. For them it was obvious that he was at fault, otherwise why would so many terrible afflictions have befallen him? Iyov, however, insisted that he has not sinned, and challenged God as to why he had been made to endure such terrible miseries, since he was innocent! God responded that He knew this to be true, but confronted Iyov with a question which speaks to the core of the matter: *Where were you when I laid the foundations of the earth?*[2] In other words: Since when is the human being really the measure of all things? The universe with its black holes, galaxies, and trillions of stars clearly indicates that God's reason to create the universe surpasses by far the argument that all this was just created for our sake. That we suffer, and that natural disasters take place, may have to do with matters which go to the very foundation of all existence and have nothing to do with our religious or moral failures.

Do terrible tragedies which afflict the innocent raise the question of whether it is more honest to deny God's existence? Does all the pain in this world not make a strong case for such a proposition? Is the constant attempt to justify God's existence, by way of apologetics, not a farce, and futile?

This attitude suffers from erroneous reasoning. It assumes, as do the "pro-God" apologists, that God needs to fit the picture we have of Him, or would like to have of Him: a *good* God. However, by making God good by *our* standards, we are essentially making God into an idol, one who fits our standards and fulfills our needs. That is surely not the Jewish God. While He shares with us certain qualities, He is far more than that. He does not belong to any category with which we can identify.

It seems that God is *not* the type of "good God" we always speak about and want to believe in. His goodness may apply

---

2. *Iyov* 38:4.

only to the fact that He is good *in and of Himself*. He possesses a goodness, a truth known only to Him and which has no bearing on us. This argument is not apologetic but an admission of our limited understanding.

Creating God in our image

Atheism is no solution. It is an escape, but ultimately only increases the problem. It requires greater faith to argue that all of existence is accidental than to argue that there is a purpose and a Creator to all existence. *The believer is a greater skeptic than the atheist.* The difference is that one admits his limitations, while the other one does not. "The writers against religion whilst they oppose every system, are wisely careful never to set up any of their own," said Edmund Burke.[3]

This idea is supported by a well-known passage in the Talmud[4] discussing the case of *shiluach haken* — the obligation to send away a mother bird before taking her young.[5] In an unusually harsh statement, the sages forbid one to say that *compassion* is the reason for this law, and they declare that one who says this "is to be silenced." It is not mercy behind this law, says the Talmud, but the unknowable Divine Will. Ultimately, we do not know why things are the way they are. God cannot be scrutinized.

The problem of creating God in our image is not a new one. Moshe asks God to reveal His name to him before he conveys the message to the Jews that He will redeem them from Egyptian bondage. God refuses to do so, and His answer is astonishing: "I will be Whoever I will be. I am not a 'what,' or a 'when.' I am not even a 'who.' There is no term you can use to describe Me.

---

3. Edmund Burke, *The Works of Edmund Burke: With a Memoir, Volume 1* (NY: Harper & Brothers, 1860), xii.
4. *Berachot* 33b.
5. *Devarim* 22:6-7.

Any attempt to give Me an image is a violation of My very being. Any conclusive explanation of My deeds is idol worship. I permit you to describe Me in human terms only as long as you know that any such description will ultimately break down. No word can ever contain Me."

What are we to do?

As mentioned in an earlier essay, Bet Hillel and Bet Shammai debated the question of whether it is better for human beings to have been created, or not.[6] They concluded that it would have been better for mankind *not* to have been created, but now that he is created, he should watch his deeds. This is a most remarkable observation. The truth about this bizarre debate is that it touches on one of the greatest mysteries known to mankind:

What is the purpose of the universe and of human existence? Can we even know? By deciding that it would have been better for us not to have been created, Bet Hillel and Bet Shammai made a powerful point. There is no way to know the ultimate purpose of our existence. We have no idea why God wanted us — or for that matter the universe — to exist. Perhaps to reward us for our good deeds? Maybe so that we may enjoy life and merit to observe the mitzvot?

But these answers only raise more questions. Why did we need to be created so as to be rewarded, or to enjoy life and perform the mitzvot? Would it not have been better if we had not been created? First, we would have been unaware of what we were missing. Second, we would not have had to encounter the many and frequent severe trials accompanied by unbearable pain. Are the joys of life and reward really enough to warrant creation when it goes hand in hand with genocide, natural calamities, disease and death? From the point of view of morality, there is nothing

---

6. Eruvin 13b. See the essay: "Lessons of Religious Optimism," p. 39-40..

to support creation. It is unjust and indefensible. Yet, God has decided it must be. The reason, then, must be much greater than we can ever fathom.

Ultimately, God alone is responsible, not only for natural catastrophes, as we saw in the last chapter, but ultimately also for man's evil deeds. After all, He created mankind and gave us the capability to do evil. The most Bet Hillel and Bet Shammai could conclude was: now that we are here, we had better proceed with caution.

Questions to Ponder
from the DCA Think Tank

1. If attempting to understand why bad things happen to good people through a theological lens is, in fact, idolatry, is there any lens through which tragedy *can* be examined? And if so, what might that lens be? Alternatively, would you be willing to embrace the notion that tragedy might have *no* meaning at all (or at least not in any terms we can understand)?

2. *"Theodicy as a means of claiming that God can be justified in human terms is a form of idol worship."* Yet if God's terms are in the realm of the unknowable, then how else are we to engage with the Divine, if not in human terms?

3. When God tells Avraham at the end of Genesis Chapter 18 that Sodom will be destroyed, Avraham famously argues, holding God to account. If God cannot be scrutinized, what are we to learn from this story? Are we not to follow in Avraham's footsteps and to likewise hold God to account, even today?

4. The suggestion is made here that God might not only not be good by human standards, but even have "reasons beyond righteousness.". What are your thoughts on this? Does it bring up any visceral feelings?

5. The following is a poem by Think Tank member Dina Pinner, who wrote the above Questions to Ponder.

In God's image I am cast
In rage, jealousy, violence, destruction
Plagued, thirsty, deserted
And it is good
And enough

What creative piece might you put together in response to Rabbi Cardozo's words about God and tragedy?

Spinoza's Blunder and Noah's Misguided Religiosity[1]

וידבר אלהים אל נח לאמור צא מן התבה

God spoke to Noah, saying, "Come out of the ark…" *Bereshit 8:16*

IN HIS TRACTATUS Theologico-Politicus, Baruch Spinoza (1632–1677), the famous Jewish "philosopher apostate," launches one of his most outspoken attacks on Judaism. Not mincing words, he accuses Judaism of demanding obsessive and outrageous obedience:

> The sphere of reason is…truth and wisdom; the sphere of theology is piety and obedience…. Philosophy has no end in view save truth: faith …looks for nothing but obedience and piety…. Scripture…does not condemn ignorance, but obstinacy….[2]

In contrast, he argues:

> Jesus sought solely to teach the universal moral law…the Pharisees [who were the sages of Israel], in their ignorance,

---

1. This essay was originally published in Nathan Lopes Cardozo, *Jewish Law as Rebellion: A Plea for Religious Authenticity and Halachic Courage* (Jerusalem: Urim Publications, 2018), Chapter 15.
2. Benedict de Spinoza, *A Theologico-Political Treatise*, chaps. 15, in *The Chief Works of Benedict de Spinoza*, trans. R.H.M. Elwes (London: G. Bell and Sons, 1883), vol. 1.

thought that the observance of the state law and the Mosaic law was the sum total of morality; whereas such laws merely had reference to the public welfare, and aimed not so much at instructing the Jews as at keeping them under constraint.[3]

These are serious words from a great thinker, and we need to ask ourselves whether his observations are correct or not. Is Judaism indeed a religion whose primary purpose is to force people's obedience to its demands and keep them under control?

I WOULD HAVE BROKEN DOWN THE ARK

There is a remarkable midrash, which I believe challenges Spinoza's critique, while simultaneously proving his point. Commenting on Noah's reluctance to leave the ark after the Flood, the midrash makes the following biting comment:

> Once the waters had abated, Noah should have left the ark. However, Noah said to himself, "I entered with God's permission, as it says, 'Go into the ark.' (Bereshit 7:1) Shall I now leave without permission?" The Holy One, blessed be He, said to him, "Is it permission, then, that you are seeking? Very well, then, here is permission," as it is said: [Then God said to Noah] "Come out of the ark." (Bereshit 8:16) Rabbi Yehuda bar Ilai said: "If I had been there, I would have broken down the ark and taken myself out."[4]

There can be little doubt that this midrash confronts Spinoza's critique head-on. It seems to express a lack of patience with submissive religiosity that stifles human autonomy, action, innovation, and responsibility. It warns against the type of religiosity that is self-serving and dangerous, a concept best described by the untranslatable Yiddish/German word *frumkeit*. This refers

---

3. Ibid., chap. 5.
4. *Midrash Tanchuma*, Buber ed., Noah 14.

to an artificial, superficial form of religious behavior, which in our days has become synonymous with the authentic way of Jewish religious living. Instead of agreeing with this sort of piety, the midrash bitterly attacks it as an escape mechanism and lack of *genuine* religiosity.

Noah's Religious Self-Deception

In our story, Noah is a man who lives in self-deception, believing that he has reached the pinnacle of religiosity while in fact he is unknowingly pretending. There is nothing dishonest about him. Noah, in all sincerity, believes that no one should make a move unless God tells him to do so. There is no place for religious initiative. There is only obedience. What he does not realize is that this attitude will wreak total havoc. It is *the* recipe for continued flooding, the termination of all human life, and consequently the elimination of the possibility for genuine religiosity. More to the point, it is exactly what God does *not* want. The great biblical message is that God wants us to be His partner in Creation, not His robot.

What does Noah say when God informs him that He will destroy the world? What does he say when God commands him to build the ark and then enter it together with his family and the animals?

Nothing!

Why? Because Noah is very *frum* (religious) and won't challenge God. Who is he to do so? And so he enters the ark with a clear conscience. He is brave, obedient, and feels very good about himself. No doubt Noah prays *Shacharit*, *Mincha*, and *Arvit* daily. Surely he eats kosher and observes Shabbat, but only because God tells him to do so. He obeys the letter of the law and will never go beyond the divine command.

What Noah does not grasp is that he is hiding behind his own misplaced religiosity. It is most convenient and carries no responsibility. All is in the hands of God. His argument is straightforward: If God decides that the world has to come to an end, how can man dare to interfere? Who is he to know what is right or wrong? There must be only obedience.

THE ARK AS GHETTO

The ark is a marvelous place — it is comfortable, there is no need to steer it, and nothing to fear. It floats on its own; one need not know where it is going. It has no sails to adjust to the winds. One just sits on his deckchair and waits for what will come.

The ark is a ghetto, both physically and mentally. It has no windows other than one on the roof allowing a view of Heaven.[5] One cannot even look outside to see what's going on around it and hear the cries of millions who are drowning, desperately crying for help. No, the walls are too thick to hear any noise from outside. The ark is a highly secure place — an oasis in the storm of human pain and upheaval. True, inside the ghetto, one has his or her tasks. Noah has to look after his family, as well as feed the animals and take care of them. But that is only because he is *commanded* to do so. Nothing is done beyond his religious obligations. Noah is *homo religiosus* par excellence. His is the ark of total obedience. It is against just this type of religious personality that Spinoza correctly protests.

But this is not the authentic religious *Jewish* personality. What would Avraham, the first Jew in history, have done? From reading his life story, it is clear that he would have refused to go into the ark. He would have fought God, telling Him that it is unjust to drown all of humankind. He would have contested God's decision, as he did in the case of the evil men in Sedom and Amora. And if God had forced him into the ark, he would not have waited an extra moment to get out. He would have stood at the edge and

---

5. See *Rashi* on *Bereshit* 6:16; *Bereshit Rabba*, Vilna ed., 31:11.

destroyed the ark as soon as he saw land, just as Rabbi Yehuda bar Ilai would have done.

Avraham, like Rabbi Yehuda bar Ilai, proves Spinoza wrong. Noah does not represent genuine religiosity. Yes, many religious Jews believe that it is only in obedience that one must live one's religious life. But that is not what authentic Judaism is all about. Judaism is a covenant between man and God, in which mankind is co-creator. God orders us to take action beyond His commandments. We are asked to build the world with the ingredients that God supplied at the time of creation. And when God destroys the world, it is our task to restore it.[6] We are obligated to storm out of the ark, protest, and start rebuilding.

A MEASURE OF WHEAT AND A BUNDLE OF FLAX

But God demands even more of us. We are also asked to be a partner in the creation of the Torah. Consider the following midrash:

> Once I was on a journey, and I came upon a man who went the way of heretics. He accepted the Written Torah but not the Oral Torah. He said to me: The Written Law was given to us from Mount Sinai; the Oral Law was not given from Mount Sinai. I said to him: But were not both the Written and the Oral Torah spoken by the Almighty? Then what difference is there between the Written and the Oral Torah? To what can this be compared? To a king of flesh and blood who had two servants and loved them both with perfect love. And he gave them each a measure of wheat and a bundle of flax. The wise servant, what did he do? He took the flax and spun a cloth. Then he took the wheat and made flour. He cleansed, ground, kneaded, and baked the flour, and set

---

6. See Nathan Lopes Cardozo, "God is Unjustifiable" (Thoughts to Ponder 250). Accessible online at: https://www.cardozoacademy.org/thoughts-to-ponder/god-is-unjustifiable-ttp-250/. See also "Our Struggle with God's Goodness" on page 93.

it on top of the table. Then he spread the cloth over it and left it until the king would come. But the foolish servant did nothing at all. After some days the king returned from a journey, entered his house, and said to them: My sons, bring me what I gave you. One servant showed him the wheaten bread on the table with a cloth spread over it, and the other servant showed the wheat still in the box, with a bundle of flax upon it. Alas for his shame, alas for his disgrace! Now, when the Holy One, blessed be He, gave the Torah to Israel, he gave it only in the form of wheat for us to extract flour from it, and flax to extract a garment.[7]

Mankind, then, is asked to be the constant co-creator of the Torah, making it more and more beautiful.

Spinoza's view is dangerous and misleading; it has done great harm to Judaism's image. According to Hermann Cohen, one of the great German Jewish philosophers of the nineteenth century, Spinoza is unwittingly responsible for much antisemitism.[8] Many Jewish sources prove beyond doubt that Judaism imposes great responsibility on the religious Jew. There is no hiding behind obedience. The truth is that those who are exclusively submissive are only partially in control. Obedience means taking action; it is not merely subjugation.

The detailed elaboration of the law in Talmudic Tradition should not be confused with a simplistic conception of the human condition. Judaism is fully aware of the fact that no law can prevent or solve the enormous life challenges encountered even by the most

---

7. *Seder Eliyahu Zuta*, Friedmann ed., 2.
8. See Hermann Cohen, *Jüdische Schriften*, ed. B. Straus (Berlin: C.A. Schwetschke & Sohn, 1924), 3:290 — 372 (especially 363, 371); translated into English as *Spinoza on State & Religion, Judaism & Christianity*, trans. Robert S. Schine (Jerusalem: Shalem Press, 2014), xviii, 29, 51, 54-55, 59. See also Franz Nauen, "Hermann Cohen's Perceptions of Spinoza: A Reappraisal," *AJS Review* 4 (1979): 111-124.

religious of Jews.⁹ To see Judaism as a kind of sacred rote behavior, requiring no autonomous human action, is missing the point entirely. Judaism repudiates formalism that too easily leads to a perverse form of religiosity. In fact, it warns against becoming a *naval b're-shut haTorah*, a degenerate within the framework of the Torah.¹⁰

Religion as struggle

Spinoza's assessment of the Jewish religious personality is entirely mistaken, but is clearly rooted in all the religious Noahs of our world.¹¹ It is a warning to many religious Jews who know nothing other than what we may call *negative* obedience, as opposed to *positive* obedience. Instead of asking great rabbis to solve all our problems, we should never forget that Judaism teaches us to stand on our own feet and make our own decisions. Of course, living one's religious life in this manner is not without risks, but there is no authentic life choice that is risk-free. Religion, said the Kotzker Rebbe, is warfare.¹² It is a fight against the indolence and callousness that stifles personal responsibility.

Our religious lives should be inspired by the spirit of the Torah, but should never develop into an obsessive form of subjugation, which the Torah abhors. We must make sure we do not turn into "ark-niks," getting drunk out of guilt once we leave our ark and see the havoc we could have prevented.

---

9. See *Sukka* 52a.
10. See Ramban on Vayikra 19:2.
11. Spinoza's attitude toward the Jewish religion may quite well have been influenced by the teachers of the Spanish Portuguese community in seventeenth-century Amsterdam, who expelled him. Their rigid understanding of Judaism, possibly shaped by the ideology of the Catholic Church from which they had just escaped, impelled the *ma'amad* (the lay leadership of this community) to take drastic steps against Spinoza. Still, the ban was very mild compared to the auto-da-fé of the Inquisition. See Antonio Damasio, *Looking for Spinoza: Joy, Sorrow and the Feeling Brain* (Orlando, FL: Harcourt, 2003).
12. See Abraham Joshua Heschel, *A Passion for Truth* (NY: Farrar, Straus and Giroux, 1973), 183. See also Nathan Lopes Cardozo, *Jewish Law as Rebellion: A Plea for Religious Authenticity and Halachic Courage* (Jerusalem: Urim Publications, 2018), introduction.

Questions to Ponder
from the DCA Think Tank

1. What are the limits of obedience to divine will? Both the midrash about Noah's passivity before God and the story of Avraham's argument with God seem to point to a clear limit to obedience: when God's command runs counter to our moral compass, Jewish tradition seems to rule in favor of standing up to God. How has this idea played out in the evolution of Jewish Law? Can you think of laws from the Torah that have been nullified by later authorities on the basis of moral considerations?

2. A guiding principle in the development of Halacha is the notion of *sayyag*—a fence or "buffer zone" around a possible source of transgression. This has been extended to the point that much of modern Halacha aims at distancing the observant Jew from any possible situation in which he or she might transgress. Do you think this is a healthy thing? How might this tie into the debate raging in educational circles about "helicopter parenting" and its impact on a child's resilience?

Lech Lecha

Human Autonomy and Divine Commandment

> ויאמר יהוה אל אברם לך לך מארצך וממולדתך
> ומבית אביך אל הארץ אשר אראך
>
> The Eternal said to Abram, "Go forth from your native land and from your father's house to the land that I will show you. *Bereshit 12:1*

ONE OF THE most discussed issues in today's world of religious thought is the question of human autonomy versus our obligation to carry out God's command. Which is the higher religious value: to serve God in a spontaneous outpouring of religious devotion (autonomy), or to obey the divine imperative (obedience)?

Over the many years, Jewish thinkers have struggled with this issue and tried to find some solution to the problem. No doubt, spontaneity must play a crucial role in the religious experience. But who is wise enough to know what makes an extemporaneous burst of religiosity into an authentic service of God?

We find several incidents in the Torah where humans decided to take religious devotion into their own hands only to pay a heavy price. Well known is the event where Nadav and Avihu, sons of Aaron, brought a "strange" (illicit) fire into the Tent of Meeting and lost their lives because of this autonomous act.[1]

---

1. Vayikra, 10:1-2

The controversial Professor Yeshayahu Leibowitz z.l., relying heavily on earlier commentaries, writes:

> Just as it is possible for a person to be drawn to regard the (golden) calf as god even when his intention was to worship God (see Sforno and Meshech Chochma); the worship of God itself, if not performed with an awareness that one is obeying an order of God, but because of an inner drive to serve God, is a kind of idolatry — even when the person's intentions are to serve God. The faith which is expressed in the practical mitzvot in the worship of God is not something which is meant to give expression or release to man's emotions, but its importance lies in the fact that the person has accepted upon himself what, in the post-Biblical tradition is known as the yoke of the kingdom of Heaven and the yoke of the Torah and mitzvot. Faith is expressed in the act which man does due to his awareness of his obligation to do it and not because of an internal urge....[otherwise,] this is illicit fire.[2]

A careful reading of a comment by Ohr Hachaim seems to bear out this view. He wonders why Parashat Lech Lecha begins with an unusual introductory clause: "And God said to Avraham, *lech lecha me-artzecha* (leave your country)..." (Bereshit 12:1) This is the first time in the Torah that God speaks to Avraham, so the appropriate clause would have been: "And God *appeared* to Avraham and said, *lech lecha*..." Ohr Hachaim understands the absence of this clause to mean there was only divine speech but no divine revelation. In other words, there was no exalted religious experience that would have transformed Avraham, "just" a voice speaking to him, which he recognized as coming from God.

Ohr Hachaim offers two possible reasons for this, one of which is that up until now Avraham had not yet received any

---

2. *Notes and Remarks on the Weekly Parashah*, Chemed Books, 1990, tr. Shmuel Himelstein, p.106.

divine commandment to which he had responded with absolute commitment. In Ohr Hachaim's words, "God refused to grant Avraham the ultimate revelation until He put him to the supreme test — whether he will carry out His commandment, or not." Only after Avraham had proved his devotion by fulfilling God's commandment (obedience) would God be willing to appear to him and provide him with a religious experience of the highest order. It is for this reason that the commandment *lech lecha* was not preceded by the words "And God *appeared* to Avraham." The Torah indeed informs us (12:7) that God did actually appear to Avraham, but only *after* he fulfilled this commandment.

This may be the answer to a crucial question related to one of the most heroic moments in Avraham's life. According to a midrash in Bereshit Rabbah[3], Nimrod, the despot of those days and arch enemy of Avraham, threw him into the *kivshan ha-esh* (fiery furnace) — the first holocaust experience of the first Jew — after Avraham refused to stop teaching his fellow man about God, despite Nimrod's demand that Avraham instruct people to worship fire. Yet, why is Avraham's unprecedented valor not mentioned in the text of the Torah, but only in the Oral Torah?

The answer to this fundamental question may very well be based on our earlier observations. As impressive as this episode may have been, it in no way sets the standards for Jewish worship. After all, Avraham acted on his own. He was not commanded by God. It was, no doubt, a correct and desired response to Nimrod's tyranny, but it was an autonomous one. As such, it lacked the fundamental disposition of a religious act commanded by God.

Spontaneity, then, seems to have value only when it deepens the mitzvah, not when it tries to replace it.

However, another incident in the life of Avraham makes us wonder whether this conclusion is indeed tenable. After having

---

3. Bereshit Rabbah 38:11 (ed. Theodor-Albeck, 363-364). See also Eruvin 53a and Pesachim 118a

been informed that his nephew Lot was captured by several kings, Avraham organized an army of three hundred eighteen men and pursued the kings "as far as Dan." (Bereshit 14:12-14) Fighting these kings was far from easy and highly risky. Just a few verses earlier we are told that these monarchs had defeated the kings of Sedom and Amorah. Clearly they would be able to defeat Avraham's army as well; his chances of victory were remote at best. From a halachic-ethical point of view it seems clear that Avraham had no obligation to try and save Lot. One does not have to enter a high-risk situation to save another from death. It may be questionable whether this would even be permitted.

According to the Talmud (Avoda Zarah 25a), our patriarchs were called *yesharim* — straight, upstanding men. Commentators explain that it was their unusual objectivity and refusal to be influenced by external negative forces that made them *yesharim* — individuals of outstanding moral character. In fact, they are of the opinion that the patriarchs did not always behave by halachic standards alone but conducted themselves according to even higher moral ideals, especially when interacting with their fellow men. This is well expressed by the Yiddish word *menschlichkeit* (my apologies to my co-Sephardic religionists!) Avraham felt a special obligation to save the life of his nephew, since Lot's father Haran had become a martyr for God's sake, i.e. for Avraham's very mission.[4]

Ramban adds (Bereshit 19:29) that Lot had gone out of his way to look after Avraham, who was already an old man, and wandered with him from place to place so as to serve him. In fact, this is the reason why Lot went to dwell in Sedom; if not for Avraham, he would have remained in Haran. Consequently, says the Ramban, "it was inconceivable that any evil should have overtaken him because of (his having looked after) Avraham. This,

---

4. See *Emet LeYaakov* by Rabbi Yaakov Kamenetsky, page 91.

too, was the reason that Avraham risked his life by pursuing the kings in order to save Lot."

It may be argued that many of the narratives in the book of Bereshit reflect this ideology. Netziv, Rabbi Naftali Tzvi Yehudah Berlin (1817-1893) goes out of his way to emphasize that the patriarchs showed the greatest compassion even towards idolaters. His dramatic words are well taken:

> Besides the fact that they were *tzaddikim* (righteous) and *hassidim* (pious) and showed great love towards God, they were also *yesharim* in that they behaved respectfully towards the most distasteful idolaters; they related to them in a loving way and were concerned about their welfare since this is the foundation of all civilization....This is clearly to be deduced from the degree to which Avraham struggled and pleaded with God to spare the people of Sedom who were thoroughly wicked...and how Yitshak went out of his way to appease the shepherds of Avimelech who caused him great and awful difficulties....The same is true about Yaakov who showed infinite tolerance towards his father-in-law Lavan.[5]

These observations by Netziv are surprising in light of the fact that the Torah later introduces the law of *"lo techanem"* — You shall not show them (the idolaters) any favor (Devarim 7:2) — which has far-reaching halachic import for the relationship between Jews and non-monotheistic gentiles.

Therefore, we may have to conclude that a distinction must be made. In the sphere of relationship between man and God, we must conduct our religious life out of a genuine notion of obligation and not translate spontaneous urges into self-imposed rituals when they have no intrinsic connection with a particular mitzvah. "Extra-religious ritualism" is unacceptable in that case. But when

---

5. *Ha'emek Davar*, Introduction to Bereshit.

one deals with relationships between man and his fellow man, a spontaneous act beyond the requirement of the law is encouraged and our autonomous input is sanctioned.[6]

Questions to Ponder
from the DCA Think Tank

1. In the penultimate chapter of the Torah, God tells Moshe to go up to Har Nevo to die. God says that because the nation did not sanctify God, Moshe must ascend the mountain but not see the land. Moshe does not obey immediately. Instead, the verse says, "This is the blessing with which Moshe, the Man of God, blessed the children of Israel before he died."

   Moshe, here called the Man of God, blesses the people, though he was not told to do so, before he obeys. We then read a chapter's worth of blessings with which Moshe blesses the people and we cannot help feeling that this is Moshe's last defense of his beloved nation in the face of God's criticism. When Moshe has finished his blessing, in the last chapter of the Torah, it says, "Moshe, the Servant of God, died there, in the Land of Moav at the word of God."

   Moshe is now called the Servant of God. Why is it that after postponing the fulfillment of God's command and blessing the people without having been told to do so, Moshe dies a servant of God? Surely, a servant obeys without question?

---

6. Whether this conclusion is entirely correct is a matter of interpretation. Many new customs, rabbinical enactments and stringencies in the worship of God have been introduced throughout the thousands of years. They may however be seen as ways to give more substance to the divine command.

What made Moshe transform just before his death from a man of God to a servant of God?

2. How do we recognize the voice of God when it is not accompanied by definitive revelation? When we "hear" an inner voice telling us to do something, can we ever conclude that it is the voice of God, or is that conclusion always psychotic?

3. Can the voice of God be heard through anything other than Torah and Halacha? Is there Godliness or divine guidance in the development of world values? May we turn to world values, or must we shun all "outside" influences? How do we decide which world values are worthy of adoption and which are beyond the pale? If the voice of God is only heard through Torah and Halacha, are Torah and Halacha themselves independent of outside influence?

4. Can the understanding we derive from world values, or our changing relationship with other nations, help shed light on Torah values that were heretofore hidden from us? Can world values be part of a continuing revelation? Can this be what it means to receive the Torah anew every day?

Circumcision: Why Risk Your Child's Well Being?

ויאמר אלהים אל אברהם ואתה את בריתי
תשמר אתה וזרעך אחריך לדרתם

God said to Avraham, "And you shall keep
My covenant, you and your seed after you
throughout their generations." *Bereshit 17:9*

THOUSANDS OF YEARS ago, the Greeks tried to bring an end to Judaism and, thereby, to the Jewish people. They did this by prohibiting Jews from circumcising their eight-day-old baby boys.[1] On May 6, 2017, the Progress Party in Norway voted in favor of a law banning ritual circumcision of children under the age of 16. The so-called reason: "violation of children's rights," and "mental and physical harm" to the child.

This was done a day after the environment committee of Belgium's Parliament of Wallonia voted in favor of banning *shechita* (kosher ritual slaughter). In both cases, these verdicts, although not yet implemented by the Norwegian and Belgian governments, are a serious attempt to ban Jews not only from these countries but from all of Europe.

In 2013, the Parliamentary Assembly of the Council of Europe recommended to all its 47 member states to ban circumcision.

---

1. See Peter Schäfer, *Judeophobia: Attitudes Toward the Jews in the Ancient World* (Cambridge, MA: Harvard University Press, 2009), chap. 5, "Circumcision."

Throughout thousands of years, we Jews have become used to these attacks. We realize that much of this was and is motivated by antisemitism and a great amount of ignorance. We laughed it off and went our way, knowing that nothing or nobody in this world could force us to stop circumcising our children. We were well aware that giving up the sign of the covenant would bring an end to our people. No self-respecting Jew would lend a hand to these ill-conceived attacks.

Lately, however, some Israeli Jews have joined forces with those attempting to ban circumcision. They've established websites such as "Gonen al ha-Yeled" (protect the child), and organizations such as "Kahal" (a support group for parents of uncircumcised children, and undecided parents who want to consult with them). While the number of uncircumcised children in Israel is minimal, the fact that these groups have been established is a worrisome phenomenon.

Humanitarian considerations

It is impossible to argue with anti-Semites, since they are motivated by hatred, and no reasoning will change their minds. On the other hand, it is most important to realize that many well-meaning Jews (and gentiles) are deeply influenced by so-called "humanitarian" considerations, and begin wondering whether attempts to ban the practice are, after all, justified.

Indeed, there is a valid question to be asked. Is it not an infringement on the rights of a child, who never consented to this intervention to circumcise him? And, in truth, is it not a harmful and traumatic experience? Perhaps all the parties who want to ban circumcision are right, after all?

What these well-meaning people, especially Jews, have to realize is that the whole premise on which these objections are based is the result of a profound misunderstanding of what human beings are all about, what moves them, and what makes their lives meaningful.

To be truly alive is possible only when one lives for some supreme goal. The ultimate question regarding our lives is whether there is anything worth dying for.[2] If the answer is no, then we must ask ourselves whether there is anything to *live* for. For most thinking people, there is more to life than our physical survival, or having a good time. It is the exaltation of existence and the ability to hear a perpetual murmur of the waves beyond the shore of worldliness that give us the feeling of life's utmost significance. If not for that, we would agree with French philosopher and novelist Albert Camus, who said that the only serious philosophical problem is whether or not to commit suicide.[3]

There are values in life that surpass our concern for the mundane, and many of us are prepared to make highly uncomfortable — even painful — sacrifices in order to live by those values. It is these sacrifices that give our lives a notion of belonging, of being part of something much larger than the sum of the components that make up our physical existence.

We ask: What gives us the right to bring a child into a religious covenant, by way of circumcision, without his consent? Circumcision, after all, is the very sign of belonging to the Jewish people. And to be Jewish means to be part of a nation that is rooted in a covenant that asks Jews to risk their very existence for the sake of a moral and religious mission — to redeem humankind from its moral setbacks and to offer it hope. How can we commit children to a lifelong mission that they may not wish to fulfill? Fair questions, indeed!

---

2. Abraham Joshua Heschel, *Who Is Man?* (Stanford, CA: Stanford University Press, 1965), 92.
3. Albert Camus, *The Myth of Sisyphus*, trans. from the French by Justin O'brien (New York: Penguin Books, 1979), 11.

By what right do we bring children into the world?

But shouldn't we really be asking a different question — a question that we may not want to face? What right do we have to bring children into the world *without* giving them a higher mission? Is there anything more heartless than giving birth to children and not letting them know *why* they live? What right do we have to throw children into this turbulent jungle, filled them with anxieties and uncertainties, without giving them a clue as to their higher purpose? While Socrates explained that the unexamined life is not worth living, Judaism teaches us that a life without commitment is a life not lived. The dignity of a person is in direct proportion to his or her obligations.[4] All human beings — Jews and gentiles alike — need to teach their children a strong commitment to a meaningful purpose beyond the mere mundane. Just the pleasure principle is not enough.

To deny our children this is to withhold from them true joy, and the capability to withstand major challenges, as well as the chance to experience the highest, truest value of living in this world. Joy is "man's passage from a less to a greater perfection," said Baruch Spinoza.[5] But it is only through hardship and discomfort that one can achieve such perfection.

Surely children will always have the opportunity to reject the individual missions chosen for them by their parents, and replace them with other callings. Yet, it is of invaluable importance for their parents to make them aware of the fact that without a mission, life is not worth living.

When we object to circumcision on the basis of child mutilation (a description completely disproportionate to a small incision that takes only a few seconds, heals within hours, and has no serious

---

4. Abraham Joshua Heschel, *God In Search of Man: A Philosophy of Judaism* (NY: Farrar, Straus and Cudahy, 1955), 216.
5. Benedict de Spinoza, Ethics, part III, "Definitions of the Emotions."

consequences), or the basis that we are denying the child's right to autonomy over his body, it could seem that we are making a valid claim. Indeed, by what right are we, as parents, allowed to make this decision for him? *But shouldn't we also ask ourselves honestly whether we have the right to bring a child into this world at all?* Is that not a much greater injustice than circumcision?

After all, even with today's advanced medical knowledge, many children are tragically born with all sorts of deformities or illnesses, often crippled and handicapped for life. Others may suffer at some later stage in life, contracting diseases, experiencing violence, and even becoming victims of war and other atrocities.

Has anyone, before planning birth, ever asked their future child for consent to be born? Should we ban all future pregnancies and births, as we now want to do with circumcision?

Subconsciously, we all know that we have the right to bring a child into the world because there is something about life that overrules all objections against it. If we did not believe this, it would be completely prohibited to risk bringing children into the world, knowing full well how much harm and pain they will most probably encounter. As Samuel Butler humorously said. "To live is like to love — all reason is against it, and all healthy instinct for it."[6]

Only if we understand that life is of invaluable importance — and not merely a matter of physical survival — can we live a life of grand spiritual import.

One of the greatest tragedies of modern times is that millions of people live and die without ever being aware that there is supreme meaning to their lives.

---

6. Samuel Butler, *Erewhon and Erewhon Revisited*, (Mineola, New York: Dover Publications, 2015), 270

Rights and duties

Closely related to this is the issue of rights and duties. Western society is rights-oriented, and secular ethics is deeply rooted in this distinction. One of the great contributions that Judaism — and to a certain extent other religious denominations — has made to this world is the concept of duty. This is an essential distinction that cuts across many issues. Judaism does not believe that people own their bodies, and are therefore free to do with them whatever they please. Judaism, and most monotheistic religions, believe that the human body is a loan granted by God, Who is the ultimate Owner.

Parents, therefore, have the responsibility to convey to their children a purpose in life, which must reflect the notion of obligation. For the same reason, it is not a human *right* to bring children into the world; it is a *duty*. If it is seen as merely a right, what happens when the rights of the parents clash with those of the child? When parents abort a healthy fetus because they have the right to do so, are they not violating the right of the child to be born?

The rite of circumcision is the Jews' way of passing on life's meaning to their children, by obligating them to fulfill the Jewish people's covenant with God, sealed thousands of years ago. It is *duty* we talk about, and there is no growth except in the fulfillment of one's duties.

For Jews, circumcision — the promise to live life with a great mission as its guide — is God's seal imprinted on human flesh. And it is only proper that this sign of allegiance be imposed upon the *body*, for after all, it is not the soul that needs to make the commitment. The soul is already committed to its mission. It is the body — the very instrument through which one carries the soul, enabling one to live a life of nobility — that makes a vow to compel itself to serve God.

Like a piece of paper that carries the buying power of a certain dollar amount, the body serves as the vessel that holds the soul.

Abraham Joshua Heschel noted that, just as the symbolic markings on the bill inform us of the value assigned to it by the treasury department, so too does the "sign" that parents inscribe on the bodies of their children reveal the greatness of the souls they house.

Since Judaism strongly believes in action and the physical, not only in faith and spirituality, the transient act of baptizing with water is insufficient. Judaism wants the body to be transformed. And if the body fails to live up to its lofty responsibilities, the physical imprint of the circumcision serves as a constant reminder of what it means to reside in the presence of God; it is a testimony to one's spiritual obligations and potential. The claim that it may hurt for a moment, and that it interferes with the child's self-determination, is totally disproportionate to its infinite spiritual value. The child, from the very beginning of his life, is physically and symbolically reminded that living a life of higher meaning requires sacrifice, but is also the source of both ultimate happiness and the notion of mission.[7]

A sense of mission

Medical science has not yet determined whether circumcision has medical advantages. According to many medical experts it has, but arguing about this is missing the point. Circumcision has nothing to do with medical advantages. It has to do with the meaning of life and its higher purpose.

But what about all the Jews who are no longer religious and have abandoned Judaism? Why should they continue to circumcise their children?

The famous arch-critic of Judaism, Baruch Spinoza, provides a surprising answer: "The sign of circumcision is, I think, so important that I could persuade myself that it alone would preserve

---

7. See J.D. Levenson, "The New Enemies of Circumcision," *Commentary*, March 2000. There Levenson discusses the reason why women do not have a sign like brit milah.

the nation forever."[8] What this great philosopher was arguing is that Jews may reject Shabbat, kashrut and Judaism at large, but as long as they circumcise their children, they will preserve their nation from utter oblivion, because they realize that it stands at the core of Jewishness, and represents a good deal more than just a religious rite or the belief in God.

Circumcision is an event that exists as a moment in the past, yet extends into the future. From a human perspective, circumcision happens just once; but from the perspective of mission, the message conveyed by this act — the Jewish nation's unwavering commitment either to God, ethics, or Jewishness — resounds forever. Monuments of stone may disappear; acts of the spirit will never vanish.

From a religious perspective, at the time of circumcision, parents imprint God's seal on the body of their child, thus bringing him into the covenant with God, and with human meaning. From that moment, the child begins his journey on the road of commitment to holiness which, although not yet known to him, is the most challenging and rewarding mission life can offer — to become a servant of God and a blessing to all nations.

The miracle of Jewish survival

As Spinoza, who had left behind his Jewishness, so correctly observed, circumcision is the secret to the miracle of Jewish survival. What those Jews who oppose circumcision should never forget is that the attempt to outlaw this rite would not only make Jewish life impossible, but would probably end all Jewish existence. Banning circumcision in Europe would mean that Jews living there would need to immigrate to Israel, but banning circumcision in Israel would mean an end the State of Israel as the national

---

8. Benedict de Spinoza, *A Theologico-Political Treatise*, chap. 3 in *The Chief Works of Benedict de Spinoza*, trans. R.H.M. Elwes (London: G. Bell and Sons, 1883), vol. 1.

homeland of the Jewish people. This would be more than tragic. It would bring an end to all the great contributions to civilization that Jews have made throughout thousands of years, and continue to make, thanks to the State of Israel. These contributions are grossly disproportionate to the percentage of Jews in the world population and are most miraculous. To abandon circumcision is not only to undermine the very existence of the Jewish people; it is also a great injustice to all of humankind.

As Winston Churchill once said, "Some people like Jews and some do not; but no thoughtful man can doubt the fact that they are beyond all question the most formidable and the most remarkable race which has ever appeared in the world."[9]

The remarkable capacity of the Jewish nation to outlive all its enemies — from the Egyptians to the Greeks, Romans, Persians… and down to the Nazis — may quite well be the result of this small physical intervention. It takes a few seconds, but it creates eternity.

Questions to Ponder
from the DCA Think Tank

1. Rabbi Cardozo frames the debate on circumcision as one of human rights versus human moral duties. Even as he builds the case for circumcision, are not secular states built on the right to apply their own moral codes? If a Jew wants to circumcise their baby, aren't there other countries, including Israel, in which to do this?

2. Kashrut too is framed as a debate on animal rights versus

---

9. Winston Churchill, "Zionism Versus Bolshevism: A Struggle for the Soul of the Jewish People" *Illustrated Sunday Herald*, February 8, 1920, p. 5.

the duty to eat only meat that has been ritually slaughtered. As with circumcision, there is a "victim" of religious ritual. To what extent should a secular state weigh in to protect those without a voice?

3. On questions 1 & 2, is there a middle ground which allows for both sides of the debate?

4. In matters of ultimate religious value or mission, what limits or guidelines, if any, would you impose? Based on what criteria?

5. Rabbi Cardozo derides the description of circumcision as mutilation as "completely disproportionate to the small incision that takes only a few seconds, heals within hours, and has no serious consequences." Do you think that the term *mutilation* should be reserved for major operations? Or could any physical operation, inflicted without consent and of questionable health benefit, qualify as *mutilation*? Why?

6. Why do you think Europe is up in arms against circumcision, but indifferent to the piercing of the ears of little babies and children for nothing more important than their decoration?

Vayera

Our Struggle with God's Goodness

ויהי אחר הדברים האלה והאלהים נסה את אברהם ויאמר אליו אברהם ויאמר הנני

Some time afterward, God put Avraham to the test. He said to him, "Avraham," and he answered, "Here I am." *Bereshit 22:1-2*

IT IS TIME to stop justifying God. Morally, His ways are sometimes inexcusable. Allowing a Holocaust in which six million Jews were killed in the cruelest ways imaginable, causing unbearable pain to innocent children, is morally intolerable. Creating earthquakes, hurricanes, tornadoes and other "natural" disasters is insufferable. Any attempt to justify these deeds of God is to profane His holy name.

God is too great to be justified. In fact, any attempt to do so undermines His very being. It is trying to bring God into the limited dimension of human comprehension, which invalidates His total otherness. It is a hopeless task that would ultimately lead to idol worship, the worst of prohibitions. Idol worship is an endeavor to limit the Infinite to the constraints of the finite.

To believe in God is to believe not only that there is ultimate meaning to our existence but also that this meaning is completely beyond our comprehension. We do not know *why* God created the universe and man; to know *that*, we would have to be God. We would have to abandon the human condition and confront a metaphysical reality that our brains are not equipped to absorb. A reality that asks us to do the impossible — to utterly reject our thoughts, go beyond the shore of our reason and enter into the unfeasible situation in which God's thoughts become ours.

As long as we do not know why God created anything, we cannot deal with the question of why God causes, or even allows, so much pain to exist. Only if we could know *why* the world was created would it be possible to see if there is a need for pain and if it could therefore be justified.

The very fact that we do not know why God created the world forces us to admit that we cannot know what place morality plays in the divine scheme of things. It may well be that morality is only one of many necessary elements in creation and that it sometimes has to yield to other divine considerations. Danish philosopher Søren Kierkegaard spoke of the "suspension of the ethical" when he discussed the moral problem inherent in God's asking Avraham to sacrifice his beloved son Yitzhak.

From a moral point of view, it is clear that the creation of the world is unjustifiable as long as even the slightest form of pain accompanies it. The anguished cry of even one baby undermines the very pretext of creation. We cannot infer from that, however, that God does not exist or that He had no right to create the world. It only means that by *purely moral standards* He had no right to do so.

Any attempt to explain all of God's deeds in terms of moral standards is doomed to fail. It only leads to apologetics, which ultimately produces no satisfactory explanations. That does not mean that God is not moral, or that He lacks the attributes of goodness, mercy and other lofty qualities. What it does mean is that morality is not the whole story. The need for morality is the necessary *result* of creation, not the *purpose* of creation. In fact, moral criteria may be required to temper the severe conditions under which the divine purpose of creation had to be realized.

This may also be one of the goals of halachic living. It is God who asks us to live by His Halacha so as to moderate the consequences resulting from His creating the world in a way necessary for it to exist.

Only by acknowledging that human existence is beyond all moral comprehension can we realize how important it is to God that we exist. Not because we know what God's reasons are, but because we know that it holds ultimate meaning in His eyes.

The Goodness of God; Mankind as His image

If God, by our moral standards, cannot be justified for many of His actions, how are we to revere Him? How can we live a meaningful life when it is entirely impossible for us to know *why* God created the universe and therefore ourselves? Ultimately, we have no insight into why we were placed in this world and can only wonder why God seems to treat us like a divine experiment. What can be our purpose when we have been denied any information about our existential meaning?

If God is entirely unknowable and the reason for our existence is beyond the grasp of our intellect, should we then conclude that from *our* perspective our life is indeed meaningless, even though God knows better?

Is pain, then, completely pointless, our suffering of no value, our perseverance to survive against all odds nothing but an emotional need to see purpose in life while there really *is* none? Is God the only one who knows the story, refusing to give us any insight? And is this the God who is to be emulated?

Moreover, what do we make of the claim that mankind was created in God's image? If God is the cause of so much evil and pain, does this not pave the road for us to be cruel and evil, as we were created in that very image?

When Jewish tradition claims that God is good, even in the face of all evil, it speaks the truth. But it can only make that claim from *within* the system of divine purpose. "God is good" *does not mean "good" in the moral sense of the word* but in the sense that there is ultimate meaning to our existence, known only to God.

With evil abounding throughout the world, it is clear that the "moral good of God," as we generally understand it, is not the whole story. There must be a reason for all this evil, but it can only be justified in terms of divine meaning, not in moral terms. The unfathomable meaning of all existence becomes clear the moment that evil becomes apparent. It is in the deviation from and violation of God's own moral standards, as expressed in the Torah and felt in the heart of man, that it becomes clear that the purpose of the creation of the world requires God's "teleological suspension of the ethical." The world was not created for the sake of ethics; it was created for the sake of divine meaning. It requires moments and circumstances in which God's morality must be side-tracked.

To argue that evil needs to exist so that we can grow spiritually has no bearing here. There are forms of evil from which we are not able to grow, such as the heinous crimes perpetrated during the Holocaust. Moreover, we remain with the unanswerable question of why we need to exist so as to be able to grow. True, the Sages stated, "If a man sees that painful sufferings visited him, let him examine his conduct"[1]; and "The Holy One blessed be He brings suffering upon the righteous in this world so that they may inherit the world to come."[2] But this does not shed any light on why evil *needs to exist,* since it does not answer the question of why we must exist to examine our deeds or why we must suffer to merit a share in the world to come. All these arguments are *a posteriori.*

This is not to imply that there is no meaning to suffering, or that pain has no function and moral dilemmas no purpose. Throughout history we have seen how much these have contributed to the spiritual and moral greatness of mankind. It is through these challenges

---

1. *Brachot* 5a.
2. *Kiddushin* 40b.

that people of moral stature have emerged and inspired millions. It has certainly been meaningful in human terms. But this is so only because there is an *a priori* reason for mankind to exist that surpasses any reason for him to be moral. The latter can never be seen as our ultimate significance. It is of secondary importance in the overall divine meaning of existence. It is a by-product, albeit a deliberate one that God intended.

In fact, it is in the absence of knowing why God created the world that we are able to find meaning. To be part of God's world and play a crucial role in it without knowing exactly what role one plays, or why there is even a need for it all is by far the most profound awareness we can ever experience.

What gives life its grandeur is living with the knowledge that one plays a role in some plan that is much greater than one can ever fathom. It is recognizing that the value of human existence is in living with fundamental questions which, like diamonds held up to the light, show the spectrum of colors without ever being able to unite all these colors in a well formulated position. The moment these questions would be answered, the light would dim and the colors refracted in it would lose their splendor.

Every answer is a killer; it destroys the art of searching, the very element that makes life exciting. A world that makes total sense is a world not livable. It is endless human curiosity, which can never be satisfied, that is the drive behind all meaningful life. It is not the *knowledge* of something that gives us joy. It is the relationship between what is known and what remains an ultimate question — that is what gives us the satisfaction of "being." Lacking this mystique, one can achieve nothing noble. It is God's gift to mankind, and for that He is to be revered.

It is this unknowable mystique that mitigates our pain even when tortured. What raises our indignation against suffering is not the torment itself but its senselessness. What makes the anguish of a suffering child intolerable is the inability to raise it to the level of meaning. As such, it is the most disturbing form of "teleological suspension of the ethical." It is this particular case of a child's suffering, demonstrating the complete absence of divine justice, that proves morality is not at the core of all creation.

For us to truly live life we must live for the sake of God. Our love for God is tested by the question of whether we seek *Him* or His gifts of goodness. A God of only mercy is an unjust God. To live for His sake means to feel and sustain the ultimate "wherefore" that cannot be answered. This is what the Kotzker Rebbe meant when he said: God, I do not need to know why I suffer, but I want to know whether I suffer for Your sake. "For Your sake we are killed all the time."[3]

It is possible for God to exercise mercy and benevolence only as long as this does not violate His ultimate meaning for this world's existence. It is seemingly *despite* this divine purpose that mercy exists, not *because* of it. In this sense, mercy is a novelty because its existence may run contrary to God's purpose in creating the world. This may be a disturbing observation — it violates our understanding of who we believe God is and who we want Him to be — but it cannot be circumvented. It reminds us that God is not there for the use or benefit of man. Nor is He within the parameters of our comprehension. No reason can be given for the nature of God, because that nature is the foundation of rationality but not rationality itself.

It is in the image of this divine mercy that mankind was created in God's likeness. It is despite God's ultimate reason for the creation that mankind needs to live in His image. We are asked to undo the amoral effects of God's ultimate purpose for His creation, since the need for morality is an integral part of God's being, but is not His totality. God's demand that we live in His image is in partial contradiction to the fundamental

---

3. *Tehillim* 44:23.

purpose of His creating the world. It is only in its *a posteriori* intention that this demand can be made. Since we have no part in the reasons for this creation, we cannot play a role in its *entire* fulfillment; we can only do *our* part, which is to try to be ultimately good, as God's likeness. God's likeness is only His image, not His divine totality.

To live a life of Torah is to live a life of the greatest nobility in the presence of God, fully aware that the purpose of life is to live the ultimate mysterious "why," while never understanding it. Therein lies its meaning.

Questions to Ponder
from the DCA Think Tank

1. We are told in the Torah that *imitatio dei*, the emulation of God, is a value — "You will be holy because I am holy." (Vayikra 19:2)

   However, we are careful to imitate only God's palatable aspects. In our recitation of God's 13 attributes of mercy, we cut off the last words of the verses to portray God as more merciful than the Torah itself delineates: "The Lord! The Lord! God, compassionate and gracious, slow to anger and abundant in kindness and truth, preserver of kindness for thousands of generations, forgiver of iniquity, willful sin, and error, and who cleanses (but does not cleanse [completely], recalling the iniquity of parents upon children and grandchildren, to the third and fourth generations)" (Shemot 34:6-7).

When we limit this description of God in our own repetition, is that a form of idol worship? Are we turning God into something more relatable?

Or, is it a praiseworthy thing that we do — we use our post-facto human values to paint a better picture of God than the real one, and then base our behavior on the improved portrait. (Can something be good and have an aspect of idol worship at the same time?)

2. Is there value in trying to make ourselves believe that God is Good, so that we have something to emulate. Should we be deliberately trying to brainwash ourselves for the good of humanity?

    If so, could teaching people to believe in the positive value of suffering lead to misplaced martyrdom in human relationships? Usually, we consider it pathological to look at our suffering in a relationship and to persuade ourselves that we cannot know its ultimate purpose but that our own assessment is not trustworthy enough to leave the relationship. If we believe that God is powerful, why should we stay in a relationship with a powerful being who hurts us? In the real world, we point at that kind of abusive relationship or regime and condemn it!

3. The Talmud speaks of the world to come. But the world to come is not explicitly mentioned in the Torah. Is belief in the world to come necessary? Is it a lovely, post-facto palliative?

The Religious Scandal of Akedat Yitzhak and the Tragedy of God

ויאמר קח נא את בנך את יחידך אשר אהבת
את יצחק ולך לך אל ארץ המריה והעלהו
שם לעלה על אחד ההרים אשר אמר אליך

He said, "Take your son, your favored one, Isaac, whom you love, and go to the land of Moriah, and offer him there as a burnt offering on one of the heights that I will show you." *Bereshit 22:2*

THE MOST TRAGIC figure in the Bible is God, said the famous Talmudic scholar Saul Lieberman.[1] Indeed, no one has been more misunderstood than God. But let's be honest; it's His own fault. One day He appears in the Torah as the Creator of the universe, full of mercy and love, while the next moment He's utterly annoyed when He doesn't get His way — especially when His creations don't listen to His commands. He splits the Red Sea for the Jews, saving them from their enemies, the Egyptians, and then leaves them without food and drink in the desert until they rebel and ask whether He really exists. The paradoxes abound. In several instances He rescues His people who are in Exile, while at other times He refrains from stretching out His hand when the Jews suffer one pogrom after another. He first carries them on His

---

1. Quoted in Elie Wiesel, *All Rivers Run to the Sea: Memoirs* (New York: Schocken, 2010), 85.

wings in Spain, but then makes them undergo the cruel Inquisition. He helps them find a safe haven in some northern European countries, but subsequently allows a Holocaust of such brutality that one is nearly forced to conclude that He no longer cares and has simply left. To further confuse His people, He performs miracles during the establishment of the State of Israel, later followed by the astounding victory of the Six-Day War, only to make a sudden about-face and throw Israel's citizens into the disastrous Yom Kippur War, which claims the lives of many Israeli soldiers and traumatizes the entire nation.

God seems to yo-yo through history, alternating between fits of anger and offers of mercy. By displaying these many inconsistencies, He becomes downright impossible to handle.

The Impossible God

Who else ever had such a track-record of the most radical paradoxes? And that's not all. Things get worse. This God requires unconditional submission to His demands and threatens to wipe out His people if they don't listen to Him.[2] To add to the confusion, He seems completely surprised when many of His creations start sincerely wondering why they should follow Him. It is especially the Jewish people, the "apple of His eye," who constantly experience these devastatingly unsettling inconsistencies. They pay the highest price, and the consequences are too overwhelming to deny: They start asking themselves what they should do with this God. Many feel no longer obligated to observe His commandments. Some deny His existence, but most see this denial as a cop-out and conclude that He is indeed the most tragic figure in history, and one needs to show Him mercy and be somewhat obedient.

Such is the history of the first Jew. Avraham is promised by God that he will bear a child who will father a special nation that will

---

2. See *Shemot* 32:10; *Devarim* 9:14.

promote this God and His ethical demands.³ It is clear from the beginning that God is more in need of this nation than Avraham is. His prestige depends on it. Through this nation, He and the purpose of His world will be known. Avraham can't wait to start his grand mission, and once he has a son he will do anything to build up this unique nation for the sake of God. Who would not want to serve such a God and take on this great assignment?

Finally, Avraham gets his son, but the blow is not far behind. Not only is it disastrous, but it seems like a set-up to destroy any possible belief that this is a merciful and wonderful God. To his utter shock, Avraham is asked to sacrifice his son as a token of his complete commitment to this very God! The God, who is in dire need of this nation, and therefore of Avraham's son, ruins His prestige and undoes his goals in one stroke — no son and no nation! And it is God who undermines Himself by doing so. He appears to be committing spiritual suicide. After all, what will become of Him without this nation?

To rescue God?

What is Avraham to do now? Should he rescue God from Himself and refuse to have a hand in this suicide attempt? Or should he perhaps become an atheist? After all, such a God cannot exist! But Avraham chooses neither of these options. His total commitment to this God prompts him to make the greatest mistake of his life. He *listens* and is prepared to give up his son without a fight, thinking that this is what it means to be really religious — even if it undermines God's prestige and brings an end to His goals.

Avraham still lives in the world where man submits unconditionally to any god, whatever its demands. He is still a child of his times; subordination is seen as the pinnacle of religious devotion. Only when God, by way of His angel, shouts *No!* "Do not lay

---

3. *Bereshit* 18:10-19.

a hand on the boy,"⁴ just a second before the knife touches his son's skin, does Avraham wake up from his so-called religiosity.

Avraham still has to learn that his willingness *not to kill* his child far surpasses his earlier commitment to make an end to his son's life. The angelic messenger calls "Avraham, Avraham!" — repeating his name twice, because the command to desist and *not* sacrifice is harder to accept than the original commandment to kill. It goes against the trend of what it means to be religious. Yet, *not* to listen is greater proof of commitment to this "Jewish" God than is the willingness to sacrifice in His honor. The wake-up call is loud and clear! The impact of this message is far more shocking and forceful than that of the earlier call to kill. This God is an entirely different God. Capricious and unpredictable but, strangely enough, also demonstrating that human life is holy and may not be taken except in self-defense.

Fighting God?

Until this incident, Avraham believed that it was permitted to object to God only if He was about to damage His reputation by doing a great injustice such as destroying the cities of Sedom and Amora. In that sense, he surpassed Noah, whose reticence prevented him from protesting even when God told him that He would destroy all of mankind with the flood. Avraham had already realized that the Jewish God is different from all the other gods among whose followers he lived. To let the world perish is not what this God desires. So Avraham fights back. But once he loses the battle and is unable to convince God to leave these cities of Sedom and Amora intact, he concludes that Noah must have been right after all. There is no point in fighting God's will.

What Avraham fails to see is that while he loses this battle, God clearly encourages Him to give it a sincere try so as to win.

---

4. *Bereshit* 22:12.

Indeed, God *listens* to his arguments. When Avraham contends that if there were to be 50, 40, 30, 20, even 10 *tzaddikim*, then these cities should be spared, God does not respond by telling him to mind his own business. On the contrary, He clearly indicates that He might be convinced, if Avraham's arguments were better, or the circumstances different.[5] But Avraham apparently fails to get this point. He seems to conclude that since he didn't succeed, there is no point in arguing with God any longer. Why would God listen to human subjective arguments? What could one possibly know about God's reasoning?

So Avraham doesn't argue with God when He asks him to sacrifice his son. God may be incomprehensible, but He is consistent. He knows what He's doing. Who am I to argue?

This God, however, Who is the Creator of heaven and earth, teaches Avraham not to give up. He shows him that He is open to discussion and would have listened to his arguments in defense of his son. Now that Avraham is silent, God takes up the argument that Avraham ought to have made but didn't. What he should have done for God, God now does for him. He tells Avraham, *You ought to have fought Me. You should have told Me, "Far be it from You! Shall the whole world's Judge not do justice?"*[6] God now needs to save Himself and His mission, despite Avraham's religiosity! He must ensure that the Jewish people will come into being, notwithstanding Avraham's readiness to forgo that possibility.

God is unstable

Avraham is thus exposed to an aspect of God that is both blasphemous and ethical. This God appears to be unstable, but He is also a God of incomprehensible magnitude, power and moral supremacy: One Who is prepared to listen to man, take him

---

5. See *Bereshit* 18:20-33.
6. *Bereshit* 18:25.

seriously, and even be defeated by him! Who can make sense of this God? Avraham begins to learn that this God is tragic because He makes Himself appear as a God Who lacks all qualities of a real god, but in truth is greater than all idols.

> God appears to experience all the human emotions: love; anger; involvement; indignation; regret; sadness; and so on. By so doing, He gives the seal of divinity to the very essence of our humanity. He implicitly says to man: "You cannot know what is above and what is below, but you can know what is in your hearts and in the world. These feelings and reactions and emotions that make up human existence are, if illumined by faith and rationality, all the divinity you can hope for. To be humane is to be divine: as I am holy, so you shall be holy; as I am merciful, so you shall be merciful." Thus, there is only one kind of knowledge that is open to man, the knowledge of God's humanity.[7]

Avraham learns that to be religious is to live with a God Who carries contradictions and incongruities. Consistent gods are idols, because they don't teach one how to live in a world that is full of dichotomies. To be religious means to know how to navigate unresolvable conflicts, to be bold enough to negotiate, and to stand upright even when failing. It is in the unresolved that real life is lived. Only *that* can lead one to true religiosity. Avraham learns that a God Whom one fully understands is only half a God; because a life without dichotomies is a life not lived. The overwhelming paradoxes are what portray life in its full force and reality.

Indeed, this God of many contradictions is the only God that we can really worship: tragic, yet sublime. To serve Him means not only to obey, but also to protest.

---

7. Dr. Yochanan Muffs, *The Personhood of God: Biblical Theology, Human Faith and the Divine Image* (Woodstock, VT: Jewish Lights Publishing, 2005), 177.

At Mount Sinai, Moshe warned the Israelites, "Be careful not to climb the mountain and touch its edge."[8] How true is the Kotzker Rebbe's interpretation — be careful when you climb the mountain, not to touch *just* its edge. Go all the way![9]

Questions to Ponder
from the DCA Think Tank

1. If God disapproves of Avraham's obedient religiosity, as argued here, what do you make of Bereshit 22:16-17, where following the Akeda, the angel of God praises Avraham for what he did by conveying God's blessing that his descendants will multiply and overcome their enemies?

2. According to most classic commentators, Avraham *did* pass the test of Akedat Yitzhak. This essay claims not. Is there a way to reconcile religious obedience and moral rebellion? Do you believe we should argue with God, and if so under what circumstances? Do you personally do so?

3. Is your conception of God also one of a Being full of inconsistencies and incongruities? If so, how does that impact your faith? If not, why not?

4. Since we are created in the image of God, then we too are tragic beings, replete with contradictions — in which case, is it possible that Avraham simultaneously failed and passed the test of Akedat Yitzhak?

---

8. *Shemot* 19:12.
9. See R. Menachem Mendel of Kotzk, *Emet Ve-emuna*, no. 821 (Jerusalem: Yeshivat Amshinov, 2005), 529.

Haye Sara

Leadership and Captainship

> ויגוע וימת אברהם בשיבה טובה
> זקן ושבע ויאסף אל עמיו
>
> Avraham breathed his last, dying at
> a good ripe age, old and contented; and
> he was gathered to his kin. *Bereshit 25:8*

THE DAY THAT Avraham our father departed from the world, the great men of the nations stood in line and said: Woe to a world that has lost its leader, and woe to a ship that has lost its captain. (Bava Batra 91a)

What is the difference between a leader and a captain to which this Midrash seems to elude? Are they not the same? And if so, why did the Midrash state both? If one is the *mashal*, the parable, and the other the moral, the Midrash should have first mentioned the captain (parable) and consequently the leader, the moral. We must therefore conclude that the Midrash tries to hint at a profound difference between these two roles which throws light on the personality of Avraham.

There are two distinctive differences between a leader and a captain. A leader always walks in front of his followers; he is the first, while a captain is the last to leave the ship. Secondly a leader has a personal interest in his destination, while a captain does not.

A leader is not only a leader by virtue of his followers but also because he is part of the group he leads. Their destination is also his. He needs to get there as much as they do. As such he does not behave out of character. He himself benefits from leading the others. His self-actualization comes about through emotionally participating in the actual journey.

This however is not true for the captain, who has no personal interest in her destination. Her task is to bring her passengers to their destination, and in all likelihood will immediately turn around and head back from whence she came. She has no part in the group's desire to reach a specific objective. She only travels with them for their sake.[1]

Leadership and walking in front often entail a neglect of those who were are left behind. The general is unable to turn around to take care of his last soldier at the back of the battalion. His mind is on his destination, and his mission is accomplished when he reaches it. That some people pay the price for getting there is not his concern.

The captain's concern is a totally different one. She wants to take care of all her passengers and will ensure the safety of the very last passenger before abandoning the sinking ship.

It is a combination of these two qualities which we find in Avraham's personality. As a spiritual leader who started a revolution which turned the world around, he initiated a movement which until this day has had an unprecedented effect on mankind's attitudes and behavior. His devotion to monotheism and ethics is legendary. As such he was an unparalleled leader and walked in front of everybody else. But he was also a captain who cared for the underdog and who pleaded with God not to leave the wicked people of Sedom and Amora behind. While his eyes were focused forward, his heart was alert to what happened behind him.

In the introduction to his magnum opus *Ha'emek Davar*, the Netziv[2] asks why the sages also called the book of Bereshit "Sefer

---

1. See also Rabbi Avraham Yitzhak Kook, Midbar Shur, Chayei Sara.
2. Rabbi Naftali Zvi Yehudah Berlin z.l., the last Rosh Hayeshiva of Yeshivat Volozhin,

HaYashar", the "book of those who are straight." His response tells us a great deal about the Jewish view of leadership:

> The reason for this is on account of the great praise which the Torah bestows on the patriarchs. They were not only righteous and pious in ways far above the norm, but also uncompromising when it came to straightforwardness and honesty. The patriarchs dealt pleasantly with the most heinous idol worshipers of their days and were concerned with their welfare. This we can see in the case of Avraham, who prayed for the wellbeing of the wicked people of Sedom (Bereshit, chapter 18) although he hated their deeds. In the same way a man may hate the wicked deeds of his son, but still seek his wellbeing. Therefore Avraham was called a "Father of the Nations". And so we see in the case of Yitzhak, who appeased the wicked shepherds who stole his wells; instead of having a battle with them, he moved somewhere else (chapter 26). Or in the case of Yaakov who handled his wicked father-in-law, Lavan, with great mercy while the latter constantly deceived him and would have destroyed his family... (chapters 29-31)

Netziv goes on to say that this is the reason why the book of Bereshit is called "Sefer HaYashar". While very few mitzvot are found in this book, the outstanding example of the patriarchs is a constant reminder of what is demanded from Jews: an ongoing concern even for the wicked. This does not mean that one should not fight the wicked when they become a real threat. Not to do so is clearly forbidden. Even Avraham waged a war against several wicked kings and killed them (chapter 14), but at the same time he revealed an unusual sensitivity for even the wicked once he established that they did not constitute a real threat.

---

the most prestigious Talmudic Institution of Eastern Europe before the second World War.

Simultaneously Avraham was a leader who shared in some of the goals of his generation and showed them the way in their own personal lives. Above all, however, he was the man who traveled with his passengers, often getting involved in issues in which he was not instrumental and had no wish to be. On such occasions he was as selfless as a captain.

To be a Jewish leader is to be a captain as well.

Questions to Ponder
from the DCA Think Tank

1. Rabbi Cardozo writes of Avraham: "While his eyes were focused forward, his heart was alert to what happened behind him." One might see this metaphorically as being emotionally "tuned into" the spirit of the times, while intellectually striving to set new trends. Do you see this as characteristic of all great leaders?

2. Theologian Paul Tillich wrote: "There were only a few thousand people in all Europe who brought about the Renaissance. But these were the people who were conscious of the situation and who became the intellectual leaders of the future."[3] Do you see Avraham as leading a comparable renaissance?

3. Was Avraham's impact due to his personality, or due to his being chosen by God to play a particular role in history?

---

3. Paul Tillich, *A History of Christian Thought: From Its Judaic and Hellenistic Origins to Existentialism*, (1967, 1968), page 349.

The Curse of Religious Boredom

> ואברהם זקן בא בימים
>
> And Avraham was old, advanced in days. *Bereshit 24:1*

"Man is the only animal that can be bored."
— Erich Fromm[1]

PSYCHOLOGISTS TELL US that one of our greatest enemies today is boredom. Sometimes, when reading a paper or popular journal; watching television or a DVD; using an MP3 or an iPod; or posting on Facebook every hour to inform our friends of what we just did, we are confronted with the most absurd manifestations of monotony and apathy. Believe it or not, there are people who spend their time rolling around Europe in a barrel and couples who dance the salsa for hours upon hours in order to break a record. Others seek entry into the Guinness Book of World Records by developing the stunning art of eating more ice cream than any human since the days of prehistoric man.

We common people are obviously deeply impressed that at least some geniuses have grasped the ultimate meaning of life. They have accomplished what nobody ever dreamed was humanly possible.

---

1. Erich Fromm, *The Sane Society* (London and New York: Routledge, 2002), 23.

Deep sea fish

What is boredom? It is a disorder that has stricken our modern world as a result of our wishes being too easily and too quickly satisfied. Once the need has been fulfilled, we immediately feel the pressure of new urges because we cannot live without them. We are like deep-sea fish. We thrive on pressure, and without it we are lost. Since people in Western cultures are easily able to satisfy most of their desires, they begin to look for absurd pursuits to satiate their new appetites.

It is remarkable that in the last 50 years we have transformed most beneficial occupations into anti-boredom devices. Take the case of brisk walking or running. This was a very healthy undertaking until we decided to turn it into a contest in which people are forced to run harder than they are really able to. Some end up in hospital, while others are deeply depressed because they failed to break the record. While running their heads off, these people didn't notice the flowers along the road or the beautiful landscape. One could say that it all evens out, since those who won the race received flowers in the end, and this time from the hands of a pretty young lady.

Even more preposterous is the case of swimmers who try to cross the English Channel between Calais and Dover in record time. They seem unaware of the ferry service that would get them there much faster.

Of course, if this is done because it is great fun and a way to relax or raise money for a charitable cause, it should have our full support; but if it's done solely out of boredom, it becomes self-destructive.[2]

---

2. See Godfried Bomans, *Noten Kraken*, Elsevier (Dutch), Amsterdam, Brussel, 1961, pp. 13-16.

Having your fling

Even more problematic is the fact that thoroughly bored people often disturb their fellow human beings in ways that are completely distasteful. They make others pay the price for their failure to deal with their own boredom.

It has become a common experience, among people seeking a quiet corner on this planet, that after setting up a folding chair in a tranquil spot at the seashore or in a forest, intending to listen to the waves of the sea or the blowing of the wind, the peace is suddenly disrupted by the blasting of an iPod with speakers turned up to maximum volume. Looking in the direction from which the noise is coming, one sees young people lounging in their folding chairs and smiling as if to say, "Go ahead. Make our day!"

The parents of these teenagers will say that it disturbs them as well, but they're unable to do anything about it. "But youth, of course, must have its fling!"[3] This is the well-known excuse for children who do the totally unacceptable. It tolerates chutzpah, which then necessitates therapy for the further development of youngsters who will otherwise be unable to become respectable members of society. Anyone unwilling to grant them their fling is depriving the world of future geniuses!

It is remarkable how many parents seem to believe that their children should indeed have their fling in order to guarantee their proper development. This is even more surprising since these very people fanatically cut the grass and bushes in their gardens, understanding that otherwise the vegetation would grow wild. It never occurs to them to apply similar standards when attempting to educate their children. When reading about the wantonness of today's youth, they simply shake their heads in dismay.

Having one's fling should mean proving that one is a mature human being, as in the German expression *ausleben*, which means

---

3. Gilbert & Sullivan, *The Mikado*, Act I, Part VIII.

to live out one's potential. A particular strength people have, potentially, is to care about other human beings. Those who have not made use of this capacity have not yet "flinged," since one of the most beautiful aspects of humanness has been withheld from them.

Pocket, cup, and temper

Our Sages make a very interesting point when they say a person's character can be tested in three different ways: *be-kiso, be-koso, uve-ka'aso* — by his pocket (Is he a miser or a spendthrift?); by his cup (How does he hold excessive alcoholic intake?); and by his temper (Can he control himself when provoked?).[4] But according to one of the Sages, there is a fourth test: *af be-sachako* — also by how he plays, meaning how he spends his free time.

One of the great blessings of our day is that more and more young people are starting to realize that there is a life beyond Facebook. Many of them are showing a keen interest in matters of the spirit. Lectures on religion and philosophy in famous universities and other places of learning are becoming increasingly popular. Young people are looking for existential meaning and a high-quality spiritual mission.

In Israel, we see a large number of secular young men and women interested in studying Talmud, Midrash, and Jewish philosophy, in their attempt to understand what it means to be a Jew and what Judaism has to offer the world.

Committed atheism and religious plagiarism

Most interesting is the fact that young people are finding their way back to Judaism in rather unconventional ways. Official religious outreach programs are losing their grip on Israeli society. Much of the time they have bitterly failed because they tried

---

4. *Eruvin* 65b.

to put highly talented and creative people into a suit of armor that didn't fit them. Some of these outreach programs are being replaced by a new phenomenon: Jewish self-discovery. It is not uncommon to see young, bareheaded men with long hair and earrings wearing tzitzit; others insisting on eating kosher but never entering a synagogue; young women lighting candles Friday afternoon but not observing Shabbat — praying with great fervor and going off to a party. There are even committed atheists who will enthusiastically join prayer sessions. And women, whose dress code perhaps leaves much to be desired modesty-wise, sincerely kissing *mezuzot* before entering a shopping mall or gym.

Surely, not all of this is a sign of maturity; no doubt, in certain cases it is superstition. Still, what we observe is that many people are searching for a sense of authenticity.

It is an aversion to religious plagiarism that keeps these people out of mainstream Judaism and the conventional synagogue. Repetitious prayer is a killer when it is not accompanied by discovery and novelty. By paving their own way, these people develop a fresh approach to what Judaism is really all about — open to new adventures. They are keenly aware that one cannot inherit Judaism, but only discover it on one's own through an often difficult spiritual struggle.

The religious establishment can make no greater mistake than interfering in this development and giving advice. Trying to force one's views on these people will uproot the seeds that have been carefully planted. "You will always find some Eskimos ready to instruct the Congolese on how to cope with heat waves," said Stanislaw J. Lec.[5]

The religious establishment needs to realize that with regard to Jewish practice, many people have generally fallen victim to boredom. Today, show and ceremony have become too much part

---

5. *Unkempt Thoughts* (New York: St. Martin's Press, 1962), 27.

and parcel of Judaism. Ceremonies are for the eye, but Judaism is an appeal to the spirit. The only biblically required ceremony in today's synagogue service is the blessings of the priests, and even here, members of the congregation are asked to close their eyes![6]

In biblical days, the prophets were astir while the world was sleeping. Today, the world is astir while the synagogues are sleeping.

Blessed are the young people who are waking up! Social media is great, but it will not ignite a fire in our souls, and will not conquer enduring boredom. Maybe we'll realize this when the secular seekers show us the way. May they succeed!

Questions to Ponder
from the DCA Think Tank

1. It's been said that "Judaism is the religion that demands the most while promising the least." Daniel Gordis once wrote that Conservative Judaism has lost many of its members simply because it requires nothing of them: "Human beings do not run from demands that might root them in the cosmos. They seek significance, and for traditions that offer it, they will sacrifice a great deal. Orthodoxy offers that, and the results are clear. Liberal American Judaism does not, and it is paying the price."[7] Notwithstanding his penultimate sentence, do you feel that this failure to provide meaningful demands is a danger endemic to observant Judaism as well (or perhaps some streams of it)? If so, how would you counter this failing?

---

6. Abraham Joshua Heschel, *Man's Quest for God: Studies in Prayer and Symbolism* (New York: Charles Scribner's Sons, 1954), 134.

7. Daniel Gordis, "Conservative Judaism: A Requiem" Jewish Review of Books vol. 4, no. 4 (Winter 2014): 11.

2. "Religion begins with a consciousness that something is asked of us," wrote Abraham Joshua Heschel.[8] Meanwhile, psychologist Victor Frankl maintains that "self-actualization is possible only as a side-effect of self-transcendence."[9] Both of these thinkers emphasize the need to live for something beyond our selves. If traditional outreach has failed to provide this kind of transcendence, what means might succeed in integrating today's spiritual seekers into traditional Jewish life?

3. Rabbi Cardozo urges the religious establishment not to stand in the way of young people seeking new ways to experience Judaism: "By paving their own way, these people develop a fresh approach to what Judaism is really all about...." But how is refusing to step in different from the behavior of parents who dismiss their children's misbehavior as a "youthful fling" and "turn chutzpah into necessary therapy?"

4. Like most religions, Judaism maintains that closeness to God requires a suspension of our autonomy. What is peculiarly Jewish, however, is that Judaism builds this suspension of autonomy into daily life. By limiting what we eat, how we dress, and when we create or desist from creating, Halacha provides a framework in which we can connect with God through the mundane. But Halacha too can succumb to "religious boredom," becoming perfunctory and lacking in conviction. What means can be used to infuse observance with enthusiasm? Are their particular mitzvot or other aspects of Jewish life that "ignite a fire in your soul" and makes make you feel that what you do matters?

---

8. Abraham Joshua Heschel, *God in Search of Man: A Philosophy of Judaism* (New York: Farrar, Straus and Cudahy, 1955), 162.
9. Viktor E. Frankl, *Man's Search For Meaning* (New York: Pocket Books, 1984), 133.

How Old Would You Be If You Didn't Know Your Age?

ויהיו חיי שרה מאה שנה ועשרים
שנה ושבע שנים שני חיי שרה

Sarah's lifetime — the span of Sarah's life — came to one hundred and twenty-seven years. *Bereshit 23:1*

"How nice it is to do nothing and afterwards to take a rest." — *Dutch proverb*

A FAMOUS MIDRASH comments on the Sarah's advanced age: "At 100 years old, she was as innocent as a 20 year-old, and as beautiful as a 7 year old."[1]

As I watch some of my friends entering retirement, I realize how dangerous it is to "take it easy" and fall into the pit of idleness, thinking that one is at the peak of one's life, while one may very well be at its lowest point. Retirement can be a real killer, and surviving its hazards is an art. In the words of Charles Lamb:

> I am Retired Leisure. I am to be met with in trim gardens. I am already come to be known by my vacant face and careless gesture, perambulating at no fixed pace, nor with any settled purpose. I walk about; not to and from.[2]

---

1. *Midrash Aggadah*, Genesis 23:1:2.
2. Charles Lamb, "The Superannuated Man," *Last Essays of Elia* (Paris: Baudry's European

True, I admit that retirement has its benefits. "Dismiss the old horse in good time lest he fail in the list and make spectators laugh," said Horace.[3] Few people are able to make a graceful exit at the appropriate time. Most fail miserably because they retire either too early or too late.

Still, the dangers of retirement are not to be dismissed. It can be a recipe for becoming aged before one is old. Millions of people long for immortality, but don't know what to do with themselves on a rainy Sunday afternoon. Boredom is the overwhelming experience for many elderly people who never learned in their youth to live a life of great meaning, and now consider themselves too old to find one.

Keeping oneself busy

People "keep themselves busy." Having nothing of real substance to do, yet aware that this is disastrous, they look for ways to keep themselves going. Often, people indulge in various activities in order to escape what they *really* should be doing. An example of this is reading. Most people read not because they want to advance their knowledge, but because they want to be distracted. They seek to be entertained and to forget their daily duties. This desire, of course, has its place and can be most beneficial, but once a person's day is filled with this activity, it becomes a recipe for disaster. "Keeping oneself busy" becomes a disguise for the shame of admitting that one is really awaiting death. Many tombstones should bear the epitaph: "Died at the age of 18, buried at the age of 92."

In our retirement homes we entertain the elderly by way of recreation, hobbies and games. While this may be of some benefit, it is hardly the way to deal with old age, and certainly not at

---

Library, 1835), 218.

3. Horace, *Epistles* (20-C. 8 B.C.), i.i.8.

a time when people may be slow, but are still relatively healthy. The subconscious message we are sending is that people who are retired are also retarded. It is a trivialization of human existence to return people to the days of their childhood, when they needed to be entertained.

Indeed, retirement involves the problem of what to do with private time. We know what to do with objects, even with people, but we hardly know what to do with ourselves.

For most people, old age and retirement often arrive with a jolt. We are not ready. There are no official classes during our youth to prepare us for this stage of our lives. As a result, many stop dreaming and are devoid of any ambition. Some even start apologizing that they are still alive.

Being the regular guy

We need to become aware of the chance for rebirth that accompanies retirement. We will be able to throw off the shackles of boredom, which so many of us encounter while at work making money to stay alive. Retirement offers countless opportunities for spiritual growth. In no way should our free time be filled simply with entertainment, or even hobbies. These have their place, but they should never become the focus of our new lives. *Retirement offers the rare opportunity to really get to work*; to stop being the regular guy; to become someone special. It is a time for new visions and new dreams. It is a period when we can attain lofty values, to try to achieve *midot tovot* (sublime characteristics). We are by now rich in perspective, aware of the pitfalls of failure, and we have insights that we missed in our youth. Above all, we now have the time to train in undoing the follies that have become habit throughout our lives. "Nothing gives rest but the sincere search for truth."[4]

---

4. Blaise Pascal, *Pensées*, no. 907.

Suddenly, we have time to pray with more *kavanah*, to go to synagogue without having to rush or feel fatigued. We can study Torah to our heart's content. We are given the opportunity to learn the art of true spiritual living, and have ample time to do *hesed* (kindness) with our fellow human beings.

We *were* handicapped, but are no longer. Until now, we drove around in our mental wheelchairs, which glued us to our daily boredom. Now we can get up, stand on our own two feet and actually walk. We are no longer losing time, but rather gaining it. We have the opportunity to enjoy and make use of every second that is given to us. We are no longer "walking *to*"; our walk is one of celebration. Instead of rushing to a place and taking no notice of where we are going or what we see along the way, now every step we take is the goal itself. We can stop "wasting" our time because we have lots of it. It is a time when we don't have to prove ourselves in the spectacle of human endeavors. We are in a state of being and becoming. The many pressing demands from without have diminished and we can therefore tend to our spiritual demands from within.

Dogmatic attitudes

But all of this requires re-education. We must break away from dogmatic attitudes, which dictate that people in their old age are educationally dead, unmovable, and too tired to create a revolution in themselves. The reverse is true. With all their years of experience the elderly are able to cash in as never before. Nothing is more dangerous to retirement than retiring.

Since its earliest days, Jewish Tradition has instilled in people a healthy anticipation for retirement. It has created in its followers an "early retirement plan" by giving them a taste of its joy while they are still young.

The celebration of Shabbat is a great example. On that day, we already live a life of meaningful retirement. It is a day of contemplation and prayer; of meals during which one discusses, not finances, but matters of spirituality; of Torah study; of what life is really all about. He even learns how to live without a car, so that when the time comes to retire from this vehicle, he will be able to not only endure it, but to actually enjoy it! On Shabbat, he unlearns his dependence on all instruments of technology, which in his later years he may no longer be able to use.

Another example is the practice of family purity. By the time one's sexual libido has waned, he has already learned that marriage is much more than just a physical relationship, since in his younger years he had to observe the laws of family purity, which teach human beings to love one another, even when they may not touch each other.[5]

All in all, retirement is a once-in-a-lifetime chance to start living. So, spread the word and live accordingly!

How old would you be if you did not know how old you are?

Questions to Ponder
from the DCA Think Tank

1. If "youth is wasted on the young," might seniority be wasted on the aged? Discuss why, and why not.

2. Consider why a life of recreation and entertainment is disastrous. What should fill our lives instead?

3. A phrase sung in the Hallel says, "The dead do not praise God."[6] How does this statement align with Rabbi Cardozo's

---

5. Judaism requires husband and wife to separate for about 12 days after the start of the woman's monthly menstrual cycle.
6. Tehillim 115:17.

prescriptions for a meaningful retirement? Why is praising God a relevant consideration?

4. Theoretically, the aged are revered in Judaism. Why do you think that is? Practically speaking, do you find it to be the case? If so, how does this reverence manifested? If not, would you change things, and if so, how?

Avraham and Individuality; Old Age and Facelifts

ואברהם זקן בא בימים וה' ברך את אברהם בכל

And Avraham was old, advanced in days and the Eternal had blessed him in everything. *Bereshit 24:1*

God has given you one face
And you make yourselves another
— *Shakespeare, Hamlet, 3. 1. 149*

IT IS A remarkable fact that in western civilization, old age is seen by most people as a curse. According to statistics, more money and time is spent on concealing the signs of old age than on finding ways to prevent heart disease or cancer. One finds more people in beauty parlors than in hospitals. Old age is seen as a defeat. Many people consider being old synonymous with being retarded. There is a strong sense of uselessness and rejection, coupled with feelings of emptiness and boredom.

This stands in direct contrast to Judaism. According to Jewish tradition it was Avraham who specifically asked — even begged — that God not only grant him long, productive years, but also that he *show* the physical signs of aging. In Bereshit we read: "Avraham was old, well advanced in years."[1] The Talmud points out the redundancy of this verse and asks; if Avraham was old, surely he was well advanced in years. What, then, does one add to the other? To this the Talmud gives a most remarkable answer: "*Until Avraham, people did not grow old*, meaning they did not show signs of becoming older. And (since Avraham and his son Yitzhak looked alike) people who saw Avraham said, 'This is Yitzhak,' and people who saw Yitzhak said, 'This is Avraham.' Avraham then prayed to grow old, that is, to show signs of aging. This is the meaning of 'And Avraham was old.'"[2]

Avraham, then, was not only advanced in years, but he *wanted* to *show* his old age by way of his facial and bodily appearance. In this way, there would also be a distinctive difference between him and his son. This was in contrast to earlier generations in which people would continue to look young and resemble their children. They would advance in years, but with no outward indications, until they would suddenly die at a ripe age.

The loss of individuality

To fully appreciate the deeper meaning of this midrash, we need to remember another Talmudic teaching. In Bereshit[3] we are confronted once again with a redundant sentence: "And these are the generations of Yitzhak the son of Avraham, Avraham begat Yitzhak." Here again, the Talmud asks why it is necessary to tell us that Avraham begat Yitzhak when in the earlier part of the verse we are already told, "These are the generations of Yitzhak the son of Avraham."

To this the Talmud responds: "The cynics of the time were saying: Sarah became pregnant by Avimelech. Look at how many

---

1. Bereshit 24:1.
2. *Bava Metzia* 87a.
3. 25:19.

years she lived with Avraham without being able to have a child by him! [See Bereshit Chapter 20, where Sarah is taken into the palace of Avimelech, King of Gerar, who intended to marry her, but instead returned her to Avraham after realizing that Sarah was in fact married to him.] What did the Holy One blessed be He do? He made Yitzhak's face exactly resemble that of Avraham, so that everyone had to admit that Avraham begat Yitzhak. This is what is meant by the words "And Avraham begat Yitzhak," namely that there was clear evidence for everybody to see that Avraham was Yitzhak's father."[4] Thus, the integrity of Avraham and Sarah's marriage was divinely protected.

But this came at a high price — *the loss of individuality*. If Yitzhak resembled his father to the extent that people could not differentiate between them, then a great injustice was done to the very *essence* of their identities. What is a man if he is not different from all others? Once two people are identical, their personal authenticity is exchanged for camouflage and deception.

Every individual is more than he imagines himself to be. He is unique. Parents are not meant to be their children, and children should not be replicas of their parents. Hilary Putnam referred to "the 'right' of each newborn child to be a complete surprise to its parents."[5] Human beings should be told that by imitating, they detract from their true selves. Once we deny the uniqueness of all human beings, we breed resentment and violate the integrity of man. Roman Emperor and philosopher Marcus Aurelius wrote, "The best revenge is not to be like your enemy."[6] Above all, we must ensure that originality stays at the center of our lives, as an expression of protest against replication.

---

4. *Bava Metzia* 87a.
5. Hilary Putnam "Cloning People," in *The Genetic Revolution and Human Rights*, ed. Justine Burely, (New York: Oxford University Press, 1999), 13.
6. Marcus Aurelius, *Meditations*, trans. by Maxwell Staniforth, (London: Penguin Books, 2006), 46.

In Western civilization there is a belief that human beings are valuable because they are part of the human race, but it was Judaism that proposed the exact opposite — *the human race is of great significance because it consists of human beings*. This can be true, though, only if it consists of a community of *individuals*, rather than a herd of nondescripts.

Our youth should begin at the end of our lives

The signs of old age are marks of experience and wisdom. It is true that wisdom is acquired, not by years, but by disposition, and many never live a meaningful life, but only accumulate unspent youth, remaining permanently immature even in old age. Still, it *is* true that wisdom comes with old age. How true is Mark Twain's observation that our youth should start at the end of our lives![7]

When Avraham asked God to make him appear old, he did not just request a "defacement"; he asked for his beauty to become inward. In that way, he would remain himself with added dimensions.

For the authentically religious personality, this is of crucial importance. Religion can be experienced and lived only in a state of originality. Any imitation of fellow worshipers is serving oneself and not God. In essence, religion is an attempt to search for God, the ultimate Original.

---

7. See *The Letters of Mark Twain, Vol. 5 & 6* (Fairfield, Iowa: 1st World Library, 2004), 16

Questions to Ponder
from the DCA Think Tank

1. No matter how old you are, how do you relate to the signs of aging? Do they dismay you? Do you fight them with cosmetics and more? Or do you welcome the impressions of age and wisdom as they appear on your face and flesh? Has your answer to this question changed as you've aged (or do you think it will)?

2. If imitation is the greatest form of flattery, and refraining from imitation is the best revenge, why is individuality so prized?

3. Mark Twain's claim that youth should start at the end of our lives, after we have acquired wisdom, is cousin to the claim that "youth is wasted on the young." What would you do, how would you live differently were you to be able to travel in time and acquire wisdom to share with your younger self?

4. "Religion can be experienced and lived only in a state of originality." Does this statement not contradict the essence of the demands of most religions, and the halachic system in particular, to conform to certain religious norms? How would you reconcile this seeming contradiction?

Even God Admits Mistakes

ויחרד יצחק חרדה גדלה עד מאד...

And Yitzhak trembled violently... *Bereshit 27:33*

NOTHING IS MORE difficult than admitting a mistake, yet nothing is more human than making one.

In several places, the Torah deals with the need for — and the merit of — admitting one's mistakes. After all, a life spent making mistakes is not only honorable, but the alternative is much worse; people who make no mistakes usually accomplish nothing. Only those who spend their time in self-absorption and vanity are faultless. There is no road in between, and there is no escape. Owning up to our errors is greater than merely knowing how to avoid making them. *It is wisdom gained.*

THE COURAGE TO CHANGE

Later on in Bereshit, we will read about a powerful example of having the courage to admit a mistake. When the sons of Yaakov met their brother Yosef, the second in command of Egypt, they finally realized that they had badly erred in the way they had dealt with him 22 years earlier, when they had sold him to foreigners.

After Yosef treated them harshly and put them in jail, they recalled their behavior toward him and how they had sold him all those years ago:

And they said to each other: "We are guilty concerning our brother, in that we saw the suffering of his soul when he pleaded to us, and we would not hear; therefore this suffering has befallen us."[1]

When we think carefully about this, we realize the enormous courage and strength that the brothers displayed at this crucial moment in their lives.

Rashi informs us that the brothers drank no wine from the day they sold Yosef until they saw him in Egypt.[2] This seems to imply that during all those years, their joy was diminished (as in a state of mourning), perhaps because they were continually deliberating and re-evaluating their earlier decision to sell Yosef. Not a day passed that they did not ask themselves if they had acted correctly, and for years they had presumably come to the conclusion that justice was on their side.

Only now, after more than 20 years, did they have second thoughts, realizing that they had been wrong for all that time! This must have been a devastating and traumatic experience — one that few of us could endure. Who is able to declare that he has lived for so many years in error, and now has the courage to change his mind?

Owning up to a mistake that was made through an impulsive decision is difficult enough, but admitting a wrongdoing that was thought about for years and was seen as absolutely justified is a completely different ballgame.

Captivity of error

Often, we make the terrible mistake of entrenching ourselves in our errors instead of admitting them. Consequently, we are no longer capable of taking a fresh look at the issues involved. The mind

---

1. *Bereshit* 42:21.
2. *Ibid.*, 43:34.

is, after all, a devoted captive of our desires and personal wishes.

One must live the way one thinks, or end up thinking the way one lives. To live is to regret, so as to live anew.

Our main problem is thinking that admitting our mistakes weakens our stance in the community. We believe that we will lose the respect of our fellow human beings, and will be taken less seriously by those around us. However, looking more closely at our story proves the opposite.

As long as the brothers insisted on their innocence, Yosef responded harshly, calling them spies, and showing them little respect. Once they showed regret and openly admitted their mistake, he realized their astonishing greatness and behaved toward them with compassion.

Yitzhak's stunning realization

In our parashah, we find a story dealing with a similar issue. We learn how Yitzhak "trembled violently"[3] after he discovered that he had mistakenly given blessings to his son Yaakov, and not to his first-born, Esav.

Our sages argue that what made Yitzhak tremble was not so much his realization that he had wrongly given the blessings meant for Esav to Yaakov, but that he suddenly understood how he had for years misread Esav's constitution and temperament, thinking he was fit to receive those blessings.

It is remarkable that the realization of his mistake was seemingly more traumatic than when he was told years earlier by his father Avraham that he was to be sacrificed on Mount Moriah. Nowhere do we read that this caused him to tremble violently.

Throughout the Talmud and later commentaries, we see how the sages did not shy away from admitting a mistake. A famous case in point is mentioned in Tractate Shabbat:

---

3. *Bereshit* 27:33.

> When Rabbi Dimi came, he said in the name of Rabbi Yochanan: "How do we know that woven [material] of whatever size is [liable to become] ritually unclean? From the *tzitz* [the head plate worn by the High Priest]." Said Abaye to him: "Was then the *tzitz* woven? But it was taught: The *tzitz* was a kind of golden plate, two fingers wide and it stretched around [the forehead] from ear to ear... And Rabbi Eliezer son of Rabbi Yose said: I saw it in the city of Rome [where it was taken after the destruction of the Temple, and it was indeed made of gold]..." When Rabbi Dimi went up to Nehardea, he sent word: "The things that I told you were erroneous."[4]

Rabbi Dimi admitted his mistake. The importance of this admission is borne out by the fact that the Talmud took the time to record it!

My sons have defeated Me

This may well be the reason why even God sometimes makes a "mistake." In a famous passage in the Talmud,[5] we read that the sages decided a certain law against the opinion of Rabbi Eliezer who was known to be the sharpest mind of his day and was fully supported by God:

> On that day Rabbi Eliezer brought every imaginable argument, but they [the Sages] did not accept them. He said to them: "If the law is as I say, let this carob tree prove it." Thereupon the carob tree was torn [miraculously] a hundred cubits out of its place [proving that God was on his side] — others say it was four hundred cubits! "No proof can be brought from a carob tree," they retorted. Again he said to them: "If the law is as I say, let this stream of water prove it," whereupon the

---

4. *Shabbat* 63b.
5. *Bava Metzia* 59b.

stream of water flowed backwards. "No proof can be brought from a stream of water," they rejoined. Again he argued: "If the law is as I say, let the walls of this classroom prove it," whereupon the walls inclined to fall. But Rabbi Yehoshua rebuked them [the walls], saying: "When scholars are engaged in a halachic dispute, why do you interfere?" Hence they did not fall, in honor of Rabbi Yehoshua. Nor did they resume their upright position, in honor of Rabbi Eliezer; and they are still standing thus inclined. Again he said to them: "If the law is as I say, let it be proved from Heaven," whereupon a heavenly voice cried out: "Why do you dispute with Rabbi Eliezer, seeing that in all matters the law is as he says!" But, Rabbi Yehoshua arose and exclaimed: "It [the law] is not in heaven."[6] What is meant by this? Rabbi Yirmiyahu said: "It means that the Torah has already been given at Mount Sinai; we pay no attention to a heavenly voice, because You, God, have long since written in the Torah at Mount Sinai (*Shemot* 23:2.): One must incline after the majority."

This remarkable story raises many questions: Why did God not agree with Rabbi Yehoshua? He had clearly stated in His own Torah that when opinions conflicted, one should follow the majority of the sages and no longer rely on any heavenly voice. Why did He deliberately try to confuse the sages by giving His opinion against His own instructions?

One way of looking at it is that God decided to give the impression that He had made a mistake when saying that Rabbi Eliezer was right and the sages wrong! This is borne out by the continuation of the story:

> Rabbi Nathan met Eliyahu [the prophet, who is considered to be immortal] and asked him: "What did the Holy One,

---

6. *Devarim* 30:12.

Blessed be He, do at that moment [when Rabbi Yehoshua declared that he would not obey His heavenly voice]?" He replied, "He smiled [with joy], saying, My sons have defeated Me, My sons have defeated Me."[7]

Indeed, when God, the ultimate Source of wisdom, admits His "mistakes," we can rest assured that it is nothing less than honorable to act similarly. God risked His reputation of being all-knowing. Instead of fearing a loss of prestige, He felt that admitting His mistakes only enhanced His dignity.

Even more astonishing is the observation in the Talmud that God brought a *hatat* (sin offering) *on His own behalf* to atone for His having diminished the size of the moon.[8]

Nothing more needs to be said.

Questions to Ponder
from the DCA Think Tank

1. A key message of this essay is the wisdom and greatness that comes in admitting one's mistakes. Many times our mistakes cause pain and suffering to others. However, in all the examples brought, the notion of regret in having made the error is not clear. Nor does the one having made the mistake ask for forgiveness directly, in case pain and suffering may have been inflicted on another as a result. For example, Yosef's brothers never ask for forgiveness directly (see Bereshit Chapters. 42 and 50), nor do they openly vocalize their regret to Yosef (once they know he is the viceroy)

---

7. Ibid.
8. *Chullin* 60b; *Shavuot* 9a.

and the possible pain this must have caused him. Do you think that admitting a mistake is therefore sufficient for gaining wisdom from the experience, or does it need to be accompanied by a sense of regret and possibly an apology to those who might have been hurt because of it?

2. Dale Carnegie is quoted as saying, "The successful man will profit from his mistakes and try again in a different way." To what degree do you think admitting failure is necessary to success?

3. Can you think of an incident in your life in which you made a mistake and then later admitted it? What was the wisdom gained?

Vayetze

The Art of Prayer

ויפגע במקום וילן שם...

He encountered a certain place and
he slept there... *Bereshit 28:11*

יעקב תקן תפלת ערבית שנאמר (בראשית כח,
יא) ויפגע במקום וילן שם ואין פגיעה אלא תפלה
שנאמר (ירמיהו ז, טז) ואתה אל תתפלל בעד העם
הזה ואל תשא בעדם רנה ותפלה ואל תפגע בי

Yaakov instituted the evening prayer, as it is said, *(Bereshit 28:11)* "He encountered a certain place and slept there..." and "encountered" is prayer, as it is said, *(Yermiyahu 7:16)* "As for you, do not pray for this people, do not raise a cry of prayer on their behalf, do not plead *(tifga)* with Me." *Brachot 27b*

PRAYER IS BY far one of the greatest gifts that God has bestowed on man. It enables us to surpass ourselves; to see the world from God's perspective; to stand still and consider our lives anew; and to create a sense of uneasiness within us. It asks us to realize that there is much more to our lives than the bread we eat and the comfort we demand. In some way it wants us to realize that feeling at home in our world is one of the greatest existential threats that confront us. To live is to possess the art of being a surprised guest in this world, not a tenant. Too much everydayness, however, has overtaken our lives, and meaningful prayer has become mission impossible for most of us. Instead of allowing prayer to transform us, we have converted prayer into a means by which we allow ourselves to get used to the smallness of our existence. Life then becomes a cliché, and the commonplace reigns supreme. Prayer is now being used as a ploy to convince ourselves that we are deeply religious and do not need to wake up and ask ourselves why we exist and who we are.

Even those who are used to going to synagogue three times a day must ask themselves whether the words they utter can be called genuine prayer. Most of us aren't even aware that there's a problem because habitual prayer hides the actual art of praying. Too often, our prayer is not much more than the repetition of words as they appear in the prayer book, without the understanding of what they wish to convey.

That being the case, one must ask why tens of thousands of religious and not-so-religious Jews are prepared to go to synagogue and repeat, year after year, the same words that by now are boring for most of them. The fact that they continue to attend synagogue is something of a miracle. What is there in the human spirit that moves them to do so?

Mankind is *homo religiosus*. Ontologically, his very being is made from a substance that moves him to pray. This is true not only about the religious person but even the atheist. All expressions of wonder and hope are forms of prayer. Watching a sunset, seeing the birth of a baby, listening to majestic music, all elicit from us a need to express wonder and astonishment, which are really forms of praise. Hoping for a good ending, a better future, and the restoring of one's of health are all forms of prayer, even if they are directed not to God but to nature, or even a nonentity. The deepest feelings in one's life are often expressed in one utterance: "Wow"! Or, "Please let it end well."

There is no escape from prayer.

When the religious person prays, he or she knows that behind the words of his repeated daily prayers there is a world that he doesn't want to let go of, though he feels he has lost it entirely. He intuitively knows that there is a vast landscape of deep content behind these prayers. He no longer lives there, but he bathes in its light. And so he says words that transcend him, because he's aware that they have great meaning though he is no longer connected to them.

The Chutzpah of Prayer

How do we dare to speak to God, the Master of the Universe? The presumption that we can just open our mouths and believe that God will listen to us is unrivaled impertinence. When someone wishes to get an audience with the Queen, much paperwork has to be done, many meetings are held by ministers and officials, and security issues are considered. After all that, maybe he'll be granted an audience in Buckingham Palace; and then, only for a few minutes. But when speaking to the Lord of the Universe, religious people are of the opinion that they can just walk into the inner chambers of the King's palace. Moreover, they don't even need to come to the royal palace. They take it for granted that the King will come to them in their homes, and even their bedrooms, where they stand before Him in their nightwear. The implications of all this defy the imagination!

Goethe, the great German poet, said: "He who praises another places himself on the other's level." Indeed, what right has man to praise God?

We don't really know the answer to this question. Perhaps we are like the atheist who said he praised God every day because it was the only way to convince himself that he was not God.

The question, however, is so strong that the Jewish tradition has devised two ways for the praying person to escape this problem so as to avoid embarrassing himself. The first is to hide behind Avraham, Yitzhak, Yaakov, Sarah, Rivkah, Rachel and Leah. It was they who invented prayer and believed it was legitimate despite its impertinence. Apparently, they knew something that we don't — something that called for praising God. Our defense is therefore clear: We are not the instigators. We are just continuing a conversation of more than 4,000 years. Don't hold us responsible. We didn't start it! If not for these men and women, who were closer to You and greater than we are, we would not have dared utter a word of praise to You.

The second means of escape is to hide behind each other. Our most important prayers of praise are recited with a minyan. We only dare to open our mouths if we feel that we are not standing alone before the King of the Universe, presumptuously expressing our praise. In the company of the community, strengthened by our feelings of solidarity and brotherhood, we dare speak to God. A minyan is a city of refuge and a compromise to human weakness. We hide behind each other because we are afraid of being exposed.

What Can We Say?

It is one thing to dare to pray, but quite another to know what to say. When a delegation is invited to see the prime minister in order to convey the importance of certain community needs, many hours of preparation and careful deliberation precede the actual meeting. Every word and every sentence counts.

How much more consideration should be given to every word before one approaches the King of all kings! To utter the appropriate word requires great profundity. But who is knowledgeable in this? Only those well versed in the art of idiom and phraseology, who know the inner chambers of the human heart in all its purity.

Not everything that comes out of our mouths should reach the ear of God. Which praises and requests are noble and worthy enough? While biblical man was highly skilled in this art, it became an impossible task for modern man. Too much ego permeated his petitions — and even his praises — until it became so embarrassing that something drastic had to be done. A rescue operation had to be initiated, to pull us out of this abyss. Ladders and cranes were brought in, scaffoldings were erected to prevent us from sinking so deeply into our narcissistic swamp that we would ultimately succumb and no longer be able to say anything to God.

And so the prayer book was born. Modern man lacks the vocabulary to say what is in his heart, and even what *should* be in his heart.

Prayer as dream

Was Yaakov's dream of a ladder fixed to the earth with its top in heaven a form of prayer? Certainly the dream changed his priorities!

Fixed prayers may also be such dreams. They tell us where our priorities should lie and what we should be dreaming of. When we pray that God's greatness be recognized by all of mankind, or that the Temple be rebuilt; when we pray for purity in our hearts, or for the mashiach's arrival, we may say the words, but when looking into our hearts we realize that these matters are not at the core of our lives. They may lie somewhere hidden in our subconscious, but we no longer dream about them because our day-to-day needs have become our priority. Due to our shortsightedness, we cannot see the forest for the trees. We live in a state of spiritual slumber, and these "dream prayers" wake us up. They inform us that we're on the wrong track and have lost those priorities that should make our lives more meaningful and distinct.

Borrowing Mozart's notes

Is it possible for one standard set of prayers to express the inner lives of hundreds of thousands of people, male and female, each one psychologically and emotionally unique, spanning centuries?

The prayer book is meant to be a volume not of words but of musical notes. When a great musician plays Mozart, he doesn't actually play "Mozart"; rather, he borrows Mozart's notes and plays his own music on these notes. He releases Mozart's musical notes from their confinement and carries them beyond themselves.

The praying person plays his inner symphony on the musical notes of Israel's great composers, its Sages. Gifted musicians involved in their orchestral score not only bind their audiences to heavenly spheres; they inspire each other to discover new dimensions of their own souls as well. Similarly, participants in community prayer play the serenades of their souls, which, through a moment of artistic symbiosis, evoke previously unknown worlds in the hearts of their fellow participants.

Prayer as preparation for prayer

What if the inner music of the soul is locked up and cannot break through? Should we stop praying when we're not in the mood? What does the musician do in that case?

The musician knows one thing — to stop practicing is suicidal. Lack of practice will only make it harder, if not impossible, to perform later. By continuing to practice, he keeps alive his ability to play and gets into the mood. To sit back and wait until he's in the mood is futile.

And so it is with the praying person. His ability to pray will remain alive only by continuing to pray, even at times when his soul is cold and his heart empty of all feeling.

Most of the time, then, praying is a preparation for prayer. Only occasionally will there be a glorious moment when we will actually pray. But who is to say that the "prayer in preparation for prayer" is not the most valuable and exalted form of divine service?

The Need for Gratitude

Our ability to think, act, build, love, and enjoy can easily turn into an embarrassment if we don't use these faculties responsibly. There is indeed one inescapable question: Do we deserve these gifts? Does we have any claim on them? The shattering truth is that we cannot possibly deserve them. Nobody has ever earned the right to love, to enjoy. They are gifts, not rewards. How, then, can we live with dignity and self-respect? There is only one answer. These undeserved gifts require a response. They need to be appreciated. Only then can we have dignity and live a life of grandeur. It is through prayer that we achieve this goal. By thanking and praising God for all of these faculties, we acquire self-esteem. We convert our embarrassment into nobility.

Questions to Ponder
from the DCA Think Tank

1. Rabbi Samson Raphael Hirsch, in his commentary on Psalms Chapter 4, speaks of prayer as standing and accepting the judgment and truth of the Creator. The Hebrew word for prayer *"lehitpallel"* denotes self-incrimination. He who stands before God asks to be endowed with the truth that will influence his way of life, as opposed to the "plea" in which we utter what is in our heart. According to this interpretation do you see the believer as seeking material success, or only true belief?

2. Rabbi Cardozo likens prayer to standing before a king. One might ask whether praying from a prayer book is meant to serve as a ceremony before the audience with the king or

as the audience itself, during which a true and straightforward exchange takes place. It appears that Rabbi Hirsch sees prayer as more akin to ceremony—that is, standing at attention—whereas personal requests may be added independently, as in the prayers "Heal us" and "Hear our voice." Do you agree with this interpretation of prayer? Do you feel there is a need to make prayer more "spiritual"?

3. An open dialogue with God would seem to enable the soul to grow. But might we not lose our ability to join with the absolute, that which is greater than us?

4. Do we wish to see private prayer together with the public one? If yes, then how would you integrate the two?

5. Does the necessity to preserve uniformity of the synagogues take precedence over the growing feeling that prayer is losing its relevance to individuals and communities, or should we now change the prayer text in the hope that any controversy that arises will be resolved?

The Danger of Religion[1]

וייּרא ויאמר מה נורא המקום הזה אין זה
כי אם בית אלהים וזה שער השמים

And he was frightened, and he said, "How awesome is this place! This is none other than the house of God, and this is the gate of heaven." *Bereshit 28:17*

BEING RELIGIOUS IS fraught with danger. People are often pulled in directions where they can easily break their necks. To be religious is to allow your *neshamah* (soul) to surpass your body, taking it to places where it cannot dwell and may self-destruct.

Plato's Mistake

In Plato's *Phaedo*, the metaphor used to describe the relationship of the soul to the body is that of a person locked in prison.[2] Platonic philosophy aims at liberating a person from the prison of the body. Only in that way can they achieve self-perfection. For Aristotle, although ethics and politics are serious issues, the essence of a person — the very activity that is distinctly human — is intellectual contemplation of eternal truth. The highest human

---

1. This essay was originally published in Nathan Lopes Cardozo, *Jewish Law as Rebellion: A Plea for Religious Authenticity and Halachic Courage* (Jerusalem: Urim Publications, 2018), chap. 20.
2. Plato, Phaedo, 81e. See also the introduction in *Plato's Phaedo*, trans. Eva Brann, Peter Kalkavage, and Eric Salem (Newburyport, MA: Focus Publishing, 1998), 3.

achievement lies in the privacy of one's thoughts. Its content has no practical human benefit. The most exalted human being is the philosopher, who must be free of the body's demands, because they interfere with contemplation.

In Judaism, this is not what life is all about. According to biblical thought, the body is not perceived as being in conflict with the soul. It is not an obstacle, but a most welcome companion. Otherwise, what is the purpose of the body? Just to be a nuisance that one would be better off without? Jewish thought holds that it can't be God's intention to create the human body simply to deliberately frustrate us. True, the body may sometimes pose challenges, but ultimately this is to allow the *complete* human being, not just the soul, to grow. The purpose of human beings is not to dwell in Heaven and contemplate, but to act with their bodies and bring Heaven down to the material realm in order to transform the world into a better place. The meaning of life is to be effectively realized by bringing about the inter-penetration of the soul and the body.

A COMBINED EFFORT

The mind of a human — the custodian of all spiritual and ethical values — is, on its own, incapable of action. On the other hand, all the forces and energy in the body are intrinsically indifferent to ethical or spiritual concepts. Only in a combined effort of mind and body can we build the world. Everything that we do must be able to permeate our thoughts, and everything that we think must find a way into our bodies. While this might very well lead to disaster, it can also bring us to an exalted state of life. This is the task and challenge for which we were created.

Knowledge alone is never a cause for action. Western civilization has mistakenly believed that it is possible to educate the body by reasoning with it, and so it persisted in speaking to the mind, but never really reached the body. This has led to disastrous consequences. Many philosophers have delivered themselves into the hands of evil as a result.

The distinction between body and soul is similar to a difference in organic functioning; it does not reflect the radical dualism that is implicit in Plato's prison metaphor.

Mysterium tremendum et fascinans

Perhaps the most acute case of a man nearly losing his body to the perils of religion is that of Yaakov. He falls asleep and dreams of a ladder on which angels ascend and descend.[3] The top of the ladder reaches Heaven, and God stands over it. The great German Lutheran thinker, Rudolf Otto (1869-1937), called this the experience of the "numinous" — "a non-rational, non-sensory experience or feeling whose primary and immediate object is outside the self."[4] This feeling consists of a *mysterium tremendum et fascinans* — an awe-inspiring and fascinating mystery; an altogether otherworldly experience of an objective presence that generates wonder, fear, and dependence, but also enormous spiritual vitality.

This, says Otto, is what Yaakov experiences when he falls asleep and dreams. There is no greater religious moment than this. It is an unprecedented encounter with God. But it is also extremely dangerous. The experience is so overwhelming that Yaakov runs the risk of losing his body. The dream carries him to Heaven, a place where his body cannot dwell. It is paralyzed and nearly eliminated.

Just before his soul leaves his body, against all expectations, and as if through a miracle, Yaakov wakes up. His reaction is most telling: "Behold, God is in this place and I did not know

---

3. *Bereshit* 28:11-12.
4. Rudolf Otto, *The Idea of the Holy*, trans. John W. Harvey (NY: Oxford University Press, 1958), 10-11.

it."⁵ This is an instant of ultimate crisis. It is tremendous to have a religious moment, but what happens when it is too much to handle? *What am I going to do in the real world with this flash of intense unparalleled revelation?*

THE NEED FOR THE MUNDANE

The biggest problem is not the moment itself, but how to keep it alive and take it with us throughout the rest of our lives, in a way that is beneficial. And if we can't, what then is the purpose of this moment? Not only will it fade into oblivion, but it will be a trauma that will haunt us for the rest of our lives! It can easily turn to madness. Yaakov's religious experience leaves him without solid ground under his feet. Plato and Aristotle would have been delighted, but Yaakov is scared to death. *It is all meaningless unless I can translate this into the mundane.*

While his mind and soul are still in Heaven, Yaakov does the only right thing to do: he looks to the ground and picks up a stone. He wants to find the mundane, because it is there that life takes place. And unless he can apply his experience in a practical way, all of these heavenly events will have been in vain.

> And Yaakov rose up early in the morning and took the stone that he had placed under his head and set it up as a memorial stone and poured oil on top of it.... Yaakov made a vow. "If God will be with me," he said, "if He will protect me on the journey that I am taking...then I will dedicate myself totally to God. Let this stone, which I have set up as a memorial, become a house of God. Of all that You give me, I will set aside a tenth to You."⁶

---

5. *Bereshit* 28:16.
6. *Bereshit* 28:18-22.

The financial act

Not only does Yaakov root his heavenly experience in the mundane by taking a stone to sanctify it with a physical substance, but more importantly, he links it to a mundane *financial* act. He translates it into *ma'aser*, promising that he will tithe all his physical possessions. He "de-religionizes" his experience, understanding that being religious cannot mean withdrawing from this world. It must mean *engaging* with this world and giving it religious and heavenly meaning. He knows that his episode with the ladder is a slippery slope on which one can easily break one's neck. To redeem this experience, it must be established in a specific space — in a physical act, in the ordinary — not by night, but only by day when human beings are awake.

What Yaakov does is remarkable. He introduces one of the great foundations of Halacha: To give a religious moment an ongoing impact, it must be translated into the tangible, the mundane. It must establish patterns of bodily reactions and conduct, which testify to an acute corporeal awareness of a reality beyond the body. To achieve an authentic state of religiosity, there must be an element of everydayness, of the commonplace, which often includes what others may call trivialities. There must be a finite act through which one perceives the infinite. Every trifle is infused with divinity.

Rather than ignore the body, Halacha draws our attention to its complexities. Halacha tells us not to fall victim to grandiose dreams. There are limits to human existence, and it is exactly this fact that makes life a challenge and a joy. The body places us firmly in a world where we cannot survive if we don't act.

How we view the relationship between body and soul reflects our attitude toward dependence on the outer world — is it embarrassing, or is it uplifting?

Dreams and unfulfilled Halacha

It is most telling that in the Torah, the world of dreams comes to an end with *Sefer Bereshit*, the book in which almost everybody experiences dreams: Avraham, Yaakov, and Yosef dream, and even Avimelech, Lavan, and Pharaoh, too. But once the Torah is given, there are no more dreams. It is as if the Torah teaches us that mitzvot take the place of dreams. A dream is an expression of an illusory world. It represents dimensions of Heaven, where the impossible can happen — where time plays no role, where we are passive and things happen *to* us that are beyond our actual capability. Dreams that take place as a religious experience transform our world into a utopia for which there is no foundation, and those dreams have no chance of ever being actualized. They are unworldly, and therefore dangerous. They are deaf and invulnerable to the cries of the real world.

But we need to dream. Dreams allow us to be insane for a few moments. There's a need for it, but it cannot be the foundation of their life. We must dream in order to demand of ourselves the impossible, so that it becomes conceivable, even if only once. But it must have a link to reality. Once it is totally disconnected, it loses its purpose.

Dreams are also moments of anticipation — "I have a dream!" — and one way in which we can make our dream come true is by acting *as if* it is already taking place. *Halachic requirements are often frozen dreams.* They make us do things we are not yet ready to do — things that are still spiritually beyond our capacity. Consider for example, Shabbat, where we experience a moment in the Messianic age.

We are not asked to dream the inconceivable. We are asked to dream what is actually achievable. It is the Halacha that rescues us from unrealistic dreams, substituting for them others that are viable. Mount Sinai and the giving of the law replaced impossible dreams with those that are within our grasp.

Vayetze

Questions to Ponder
from the DCA Think Tank

1. Have there been moments where you experience your practice of Halacha as a way of bringing the soul into the body? What characterized these moments?

2. "It is an unprecedented encounter with God. But is it also extremely dangerous." Do you find this description of spirituality surprising? Are there ways in which you see spiritual experiences as dangerous? Are there ways in which you think they are not dangerous?

3. If Yaakov could choose how to express his spiritual experience in the mundane, do you think we should also be able to choose how we express our spirituality in the mundane? What would be the benefits of such a system? What would be the dangers? Should only certain people be able to choose? Who?

4. "Halachic requirements are often frozen dreams." How can we come closer to being spiritually aligned with the requirements of Halacha? If we never attain such a level, is it still to our advantage to keep these halachic requirements, or should we reevaluate them?

Amalek and a Warning Against Injustice

> אלה אלופי בני עשו בני אליפז בכור
> עשו...אלוף קרח אלוף געתם אלוף עמלק...
>
> These became the chieftains of the sons of Esav: the sons of Eliphaz, Esav's firstborn... Chief Korach, Chief Gaatam, Chief Amalek... *Bereshit 36:16-17*

THE JEWS' MOST formidable enemy in Biblical times was the nation of Amalek. This nation was, and symbolically still is, the personification of evil, brutality, racism and antisemitism. What revealed Amalek's moral bankruptcy was not that they dared to fight the Israelites, only recently liberated from Egypt, but that they attacked the Israelites from behind, focusing on the weak and the exhausted.[1]

In later days, it was Haman the Amalekite, known from the Purim story, who once again displayed the evil intentions of this nation. Only through a miracle was Israel saved from the hands of this wicked person.

Who was Amalek? The Torah tells us that the first Amalek was the son of Esav's son Eliphaz. Eliphaz took a concubine by the name of Timna, who then became pregnant and gave birth to Amalek, the eponymous ancestor of the Amalekite people.[2] This means that Amelek was a descendant of Yitzhak and Rivka!

---

1. *Devarim* 25:18.
2. *Bereshit* 36:12.

The Rejection of Timna

The Talmud inquires why Timna married Eliphaz, and provides us with a stunning explanation:

> Timna desired to become a (Jewish) proselyte, so she went to Avraham, Yitzhak and Yaakov, but they did not accept her. As a result, she went and became a concubine to Eliphaz, the son of Esav, saying: "I would rather be a servant to this (Hebrew) people than a mistress of another nation." From her, Amalek, who afflicted Israel, was descended. Why so? Because they should not have rejected her.[3]

This Talmudic statement is difficult to understand. It is, after all, unclear why the forefathers refused to take Timna under their wing and why they did not allow her to join the Jewish people, especially when we know that they went out of their way to convert as many people as possible.[4] Furthermore, one would expect the Talmud to justify the decision of the three forefathers; instead, the sages rebuke the Patriarchs for their failure to accept Timna for conversion. The sages' commitment to truth exceeded their love for the Patriarchs. This is remarkable. They could have suppressed the story, or they could have stated that Timna was indeed unworthy. The fact that they did not do anything of that sort proves their integrity and uncompromising commitment to truth.

What is even more surprising is that they considered the Patriarchs' refusal to accept Timna into Judaism as the *prime reason* why Israel would later be afflicted by the offspring of the first Amalek.

Sara's sin

This reminds us of a statement made by Ramban (Nachmanides) when he discusses the reasons why the Arab nations have exhibited

---

3. *Sanhedrin* 99b.
4. Rashi on *Bereshit* 12:5.

so much hostility toward the Jewish people. When Hagar became pregnant by Avraham and subsequently looked down on Sarah (who was barren), Sarah complained to Avraham about her. "Then Avraham said to Sarai: 'Behold, your maid is in your hands; do to her that which is good in your eyes.' Then Sarai dealt harshly with her, and she (Hagar) fled from her."[5] Ramban's comment is most telling:

> Sarah, our mother, sinned in dealing harshly (with Hagar) — and Avraham, too, by allowing her to do so. God heard her (Hagar's) suffering and gave her a son who was destined to be a lawless person, who would afflict the seed of Avraham and Sarah with all kinds of suffering.[6]

In later days, Rabbi Shmuel Mohilever, rabbi of Bialystok and one of the great leaders of the Hibbat Zion movement, made a similar comment. When the Turkish government was about to banish from the Jewish settlements those Russian Jews who had moved to the country but had not taken Ottoman citizenship, Rabbi Mohilever cried out and said that it is because of "Drive out this handmaiden (Hagar) and her son"[7] that the Muslims — the children of Yishmael, son of Hagar — would now cast out the sons of Sarah from their land."[8]

Once again, we are confronted with an unbending commitment to truth. Even when running the risk of putting our spiritual heroes in a compromising light, the sages did not shrink from criticizing the Patriarchs and Matriarchs when they felt the need to do so. And once again, we hear a daring statement that *because*

---

5. *Bereshit* 16:6.
6. *Ad loc.*
7. *Bereshit* 21:10.
8. This incident was recounted by Professor Yeshayahu Leibowitz who heard it from his mother. See Yeshayahu Leibowitz, *Notes and Remarks on the Weekly Parashah*, trans. Dr. Shmuel Himelstein (Brooklyn, New York: Chemed Books, 1990), 30.

of this, Jews still encounter hostility from the descendants of those wronged thousands of years later.

A Soft Spot for Amalek

On another occasion, the sages spoke of the injustice done to the ancestors of Haman. They stressed that much of Haman's hatred for Jews resulted from the way Yaakov had dealt with his brother Esav. In the words in the *Megillah*, "Mordechai understood all that was done; and Mordechai tore his clothes and put on sackcloth with ashes; and he went out into the midst of the city and cried a loud and bitter cry," [9] the *Midrash Rabbah* dares to make the following observation:

> One bitter cry did Yaakov cause Esav to cry (after he had stolen the blessings from Esav), as it says: "When Esav heard his father's words, he cried an exceedingly loud and bitter cry," [10] and it was paid back to him [Yaakov] in Shushan when his offspring [Mordechai and the Jews] cried a loud and bitter cry [because of the great trouble that Haman, the offspring of Amalek and Esav, caused the Jews].[11]

This may have been the reason why the sages declared that some descendants of Haman taught Torah in Bnei Brak,[12] and some later authorities felt that one could perhaps accept members of the nation of Amalek as converts.[13] Somehow, they felt that not all members of Amalek were totally evil; nor were the people of Israel completely blameless.

Why, indeed, did the sages emphasize the injustice by our

---

9. *Megillat Esther* 4:1.
10. *Bereshit* 27:34.
11. *Bereshit Rabba*, Vilna ed., 67:4.
12. *Sanhedrin* 96b.
13. See *Mishne Torah, Hilchot Melachim* 6:4, and the interesting discussion in R. Yechiel Yaakov Weinberg, *Seridei Esh*, vol. 2, no. 73.

forefathers? Why not keep quiet? They certainly didn't want to justify the antisemitism of the Amalekites or the hatred displayed by the Arab nations. Nor did they wish to embarrass the Patriarchs, knowing quite well that they were men of great spirituality.

They were fully aware of treading dangerous ground when they showed a soft spot for Amalek. But after all was said and done, they took the plunge. Why the need for such a risky balancing act?

Blotting out the memory of Amalek

I believe that a careful look in the Torah may provide us with the answer. The Torah demands of the Jews: "You shall erase the memory of Amalek from beneath the heavens. You shall not forget."[14] This commandment seems to be a paradox: How can we erase the memory of Amalek if we are not allowed to forget what he did?

However, it is very possible that the Torah hints here not only at the monstrous deeds of Amalek, but also at the injustices that were done by our forefathers when dealing with Esav and Timna. "Blot out the memory of Amalek" may quite well mean that we are obligated to uproot *from within ourselves* the ways in which our ancestors dealt with the ancestors of Amalek. "Do not forget" that this behavior was unjustified and consequently caused ongoing pain to this people, and consequently to the People of Israel.

In other words, the Torah teaches us to erase Amalek's memory by doing everything in our power not to give cause to unwarranted feelings within ourselves toward other nations and people. We create our own enemies, and we Jews have to teach ourselves and others to prevent this by all means.

This, however, cannot be done once and for all. It is a constant demand that should never be forgotten.

The earlier critical observations by our Sages are therefore most

---

14. *Devarim* 25:19.

crucial. By emphasizing the injustices done by our forefathers, and their disastrous repercussions, they gave us the means to fulfill the mitzvah of blotting out Amalek's memory and paradoxically never forgetting what they did to us. Not only because they are our arch-enemies, but also because we should not give cause to bring them into existence.

While the sages surely did not want to fully justify Amalek's or the Arab's animosity towards the Jews, they made it abundantly clear that our forefathers' actions had consequences.

Finally, the story of Timna teaches us to approach every proselyte with much care and love. Sending them away, or telling them that they are unworthy, may be completely unjustified and a desecration of God's name on top of that. It can lead to major disasters, as in the case of Timna.

Questions to Ponder
from the DCA Think Tank

1. The Rabbis tell a story—not hinted at in the Torah—of our forefathers, Avraham, Yitzhak and Yaakov turning away the first Amalek's mother Timna when she desired to become a proselyte. This story demonstrates our sages' "commitment to truth," but what kind of truthfulness is at stake here? Are we talking about commitment to historical truth or to ethical self-examination and humility? Or both?

2. The text of the Torah contains nary a hint of the story of Amalek's mother being turned away by the forefathers, nor of any causal link between Amalek's origins and that nation's subsequent attack on the Israelites, but, on the contrary, presents the attack as driven by gratuitous malice

and thereby earning God's eternal enmity. What theological or moral concerns might underlie such an inventive rabbinical reading of the biblical narrative? In the old-fashioned cowboy movies, so they say, the good guy wore the white hat and the bad guy wore the black hat. But in later examples of the genre, both the good guys and the bad guys wore various shades of gray, so to speak. Is there something of this in the rabbinic portrayal of Amalek, his forebears and his descendants? And what implications does this have for the way we think about our enemies, and outsider and marginalized groups generally?

3. Our sages trace the cause of Israel's suffering at the hands of Amalek and — later, the Arab nations — back to our ancestors' mistreatment of Timna and Hagar. Some latter-day Rabbis attribute contemporary Jewish misfortunes to a variety of causes, ranging from Sabbath violation to Zionism. Is there a difference between these two styles of self-criticism? If so, what?

4. "People create their own enemies." There is a fine line between healthy self-criticism and a pathological "blame the victim" mentality. What do you think makes the difference? It is notable, for example, that the Rabbis, despite laying (part of) the blame for Amalek's and Haman's hateful actions at the feet of the forefathers, did not for a moment question the people's obligation to defend themselves robustly against attack. Are there other differences between healthy self-criticism and pathological self-blame?

Remembering Who We Are

> ותצא דינה בת לאה אשר ילדה ליעקב לראות
> בבנות הארץ וירא אתה שכם בן חמור החוי
> נשיא הארץ ויקח אתה וישכב אתה ויענה
>
> Dinah, the daughter whom Leah had borne
> to Yaakov, went out to visit the daughters
> of the land. Shechem son of Hamor the
> Hivite, chief of the country, saw her, and took
> her and lay with her by force. *Bereshit 34:1-2*

AFTER EVERY TERROR attack in Israel, we have become used to seeing Palestinians taking to the streets to celebrate the killing of Jews — including children — in terrorists attacks. At such times, it is important for us to remember who we are.

While these people, who celebrate murder have lost all dignity and lowered themselves to a level of unprecedented cruelty in their enjoyment of such acts, the Jewish people should be reminded that they are the children of Avraham, Yitshak, and Yaakov. Our patriarchs would not, in their wildest imagination, contemplate such acts of hatred, not even out of revenge, whatever the circumstances, let alone bring them to fruition.

This attitude however does not come easily to us. The need for revenge after experiencing a great injustice is very understandable. In the heat of the moment, people easily lose their minds and take to the streets to carry out acts of rampant destruction. They often forget who they are fighting and cause heavy losses to the innocent. While this is understandable, it is wrong.

The violation of Dina

When Dina, the daughter of Yaakov was kidnapped and violated by Schechem, son of Hamor, the "prince of the land", her brothers were most grieved and "fired deeply with indignation," for Shechem had done "a disgraceful deed to Israel".[1] They immediately realized that if Dina had not been a Hebrew girl, Schechem would not have dared to perform such an act. He would have known that no other neighboring nation would let him get away with it. Believing however that Hebrews are merciful people, with no interest in a real fight, he took the chance and violated Dina, thinking that he would be able to use a "diplomatic clause" to get the Jews not only to accept what happened but even to agree on an official marriage.

When Dina's brothers indicated that they would be prepared to go along with such a marriage, under the condition that all the men of his city circumcise themselves, Shechem's joy was boundless. Immediately he forced his countrymen to undergo circumcision, promising them that it would be to their financial advantage. Above all, it would end the unique identity of the first Jews and assimilation would slowly disintegrate them.

He was badly mistaken. In no way were the brothers prepared to make any kind of deal with Schechem. Realizing very well what they were up against, and with what kind of mentality they had to deal with, they planned to kill Schechem and his father. With guile they caused him to believe that they would agree to his suggestion to become partners with him and his people. Because all the men were weak after their circumcision, there was no danger that the brothers would be attacked while trying to kill Schechem and his father.

---

1. Bereshit 34:7

This was the plan. But two of the brothers, Shimon and Levy, without the knowledge of their father or brothers, decided on a much larger operation. Not only did they kill Schechem and Hamor, but all the other men as well. Consequently they took the women and children captive and brought Dina home.

Upon arriving home and informing their father Yaakov of what they had done, they expected a compliment for their handling of the situation. Yaakov, however, had a very different response. He accused them of having created a Hilul Hashem, a desecration of God's name, and told them that he anticipated a war between him and the other tribal groups living in the country. The brothers responded with shock: "Shall our sister then be treated as a harlot?"[2]

To this Yaakov did not respond, and nothing more is mentioned about the incident. While this may suggest that Yaakov may have, after all, approved of the attack, it becomes abundantly clear that this is far from true.

Yaakov's mixed blessing

On his deathbed, as he blesses his children, Yaakov does not mince words. He tells Shimon and Levi what he really thinks of what they did: "Shimon and Levi are brothers, but are (also) instruments of violence...for in their wrath they murdered men.... Cursed be their anger...."[3] He indicates that Shimon and Levi should be allotted such a position in the nation whereby political and military powers of decision would never lie in their hands.[4] There was no justification for what they did. It may be that Yaakov fully sanctioned the attack on Schechem himself. But even if this is so,

---

2. Bereshit 34:31.
3. Bereshit 49: 5-7.
4. See the commentary of Rabbi S. R. Hirsch on Yaakov's mixed blessing of Shimon and Levy.

there could be no justification for the murder of the other men.

This is no doubt something of a surprise. Were all these men not guilty by abstention? After all, they did not protest against the deed of Schechem, and seemed to have approved of his actions. Why not kill them as well? Yaakov seems to anticipate the Halacha that as long as people do not pose an immediate threat, one is not allowed to kill them. There must be clear indications that they are planning to kill you. (One may, however, put them in jail or take other strong preventive actions.)

But a careful look at Yaakov's last words, reading between the lines, reveals something more. Not only does he strongly condemn his two sons, he also praises them for their strong spirit, their always being conscious of their own worth and their nation's pride and power.

This strength needs to enter into every sphere of the nation and become the backbone of the ideal Jewish society. Nowhere is there an illusion that Yaakov was a pacifist who suggested surrender.

Yaakov's point is that it is the security of the nation which needs to be at the center of the fight. It is the enemy which needs to be punished, not those who are innocent. A forceful attack on the enemy may sometimes involve the innocent, and little can be done about it, except try to prevent it, but neither can it prevent one from attacking the enemy.

The necessary fear of killing

There is, however, another most important point which even Shimon and Levy understood. There is no rejoicing in the destruction of the enemy. No dancing in the streets, no celebration or use of fireworks.[5] There is the sober understanding that killing is

---

5. The only real exception where Jews celebrated their victory over their enemies was at the Red Sea. It is interesting to note that the Jewish tradition was somehow reluctant to sing the song of Moshe at the time. While God permitted the Jews to celebrate, he forbade the angels to join in: "The work of My hand is being drowned in the sea, and you chant songs?"

terrible. Even when it needs to be done in self-defense or in pursuit of justice, it remains an act which people should hate. Golda Meir made a most important observation when she said that Jews will perhaps one day forgive their enemies for killing Israeli soldiers but definitely not for forcing our soldiers to kill.

When Yaakov, in an earlier moment in his life, confronted his brother Esav and his army of 400 men, the Torah informs us that he "feared very much".[6] Rashi comments that he was not only afraid of being killed but also afraid *that he may have to kill*. What is worse than having to take the life of another human being, even when he is your enemy, and even when he deserves to die?

When in the old days, the Court of Israel was obligated to take the life of an individual according to the law of the Torah, the sages did not thank God for the opportunity of performing a mitzvah. They did not dance around his tombstone and sing songs of praise. Instead, *they fasted*.[7]

And that is the difference between us and those who celebrate in Ramallah.

Questions to Ponder
from the DCA Think Tank

1. In the story of Yaakov's family prior to this incident, what basis would the Hivites have for thinking, "Hebrews are

---

(Megillah 10a) It for this reason that only half the official thanksgiving prayers (Hallel) are sung on Pesach night and this is the basis for the custom of spilling some of the wine from the cup during this night. It seems as though at that moment in time Jews were still in need of some kind of celebration. The angels, on the other hand, had not gone through the hell of slavery and were therefore forcefully silenced.

6. See Rashi on Bereshit 32:8.
7. Mishna Sanhedrin 5:5, and in Talmud Bavli Sanhedrin 40a

merciful people, with no interest in a real fight?" What other explanation might there be for Hamor wanton disregard of Dina's honor?

2. The author implies that all the men of Schechem were guilty of a serious, although not capital crime, because they did not protest against the abduction and rape of Dina. Is it a reasonable assumption that they indeed knew what was happening? If yes, to what extent are we responsible for the crimes of our neighbors?

3. Perhaps Yaakov's fears were well placed. Even given that Hamor and all the men of Schechem were guilty, was falsely agreeing to a compromise an appropriate way to adjudicate the matter? If there were no agreed court or mediation system in place, wouldn't it be more effective, in the long-term, to demand a fair fight rather than acting stealthily?

Vayeshev

The Many-Colored Garment

> ויושראל אהב את יוסף מכל בניו כי בן
> זקנים הוא לו ועשה לו כתנת פסים
>
> Israel loved Yosef more than all his sons,
> because he was a son of his old age; and he
> made him a coat of fine wool. *Bereshit 37:3*

ONE OF THE more mysterious rituals of the Passover Seder is the eating of *karpas*[1] dipped in salt water at the very beginning of the evening. One reason for this ritual, we are told, is to encourage everyone, particularly the children, to ask many questions. After reciting the *Kiddush* we would no doubt expect a proper meal, as is customary on other festivals and on Friday nights. Instead, we receive a small piece of vegetable dipped in salty water and are then left hungry for a good part of the evening. This should certainly raise some eyebrows.

Without denying the importance of the above, we must understand why our Sages decided to introduce the need to ask questions through this particular ritual and not another. What is there in the ritual of *karpas* that would otherwise be lost on us, and why was this particular ritual chosen to be the first in the Haggada that would prompt our children to ask questions?

---

1. The Hebrew word for "greens" or "vegetable" comes from the Greek "karpos," which means a fresh raw vegetable.

Rabbi Joshua Ibn Shuaib[2] and Rabbenu Manoah[3] give us a very unusual clue. The word *karpas*, they say, is etymologically difficult to place. Both rabbis point out that it means "fine woolen fabric," and Rabbenu Manoah adds that it means "greens" or "a vegetable," in line with the meaning in the Haggada.

The first definition reminds us of Rashi's comment on the hatred of his brothers toward Yosef.[4] As we know, this animosity was caused by Yaakov's giving a *ketonet passim* (multicolored garment) to his son Yosef. Rashi there states that the word *passim* means material made of fine woolen fabric. This statement reveals to us a secret behind the ritual of dipping *karpas* into a liquid.

After Yosef had received this garment from his father, the brothers sold him to the Egyptians. This was the precursor of the exile and slavery in Egypt. Whatever the deeper cause of this hatred, it was unjustified and led to much pain. Had Yaakov not given the garment to Yosef, the exile and servitude in Egypt would in all likelihood not have come about.

So this garment, made from *karpas*, was seemingly the primary cause of the Egyptian enslavement.

When the Rabbis fashioned the blueprint for the Haggada text, they looked for a way to draw attention to the fact that brotherly hatred was what caused the Jews to end up in Egypt. Upon realizing that this infamous garment was made of *karpas* — fine woolen fabric — they decided to institute a ritual that would involve using a vegetable.

On a deeper level, what identifies this ritual more specifically with the hatred of the brothers is the act of dipping the *karpas* in salt water. After all, the brothers took this "*karpas* garment" and

---

2. *Drashot, Parashat Tzav Ve-Shabbat HaGadol* by Rabbi Joshua Ibn Shuaib (c. 1280-1340) who was a pupil of the famous Rabbi Shlomo ben Aderet (Rashba) and the teacher of Rabbenu Menachem Ibn Zerah, author of *Tzeda LaDerech*.
3. *Sefer HaMenucha, Hilchot Chametz U-Matza* 8:2.
4. *Bereshit* 37:3.

dipped it into animal blood before they approached their father with the terrible news that Yosef had been killed.

Still, one may wonder why the Haggada only alludes to this in the form of a mysterious ritual. Apparently, the authors wanted to hide this information while simultaneously hoping that the readers would get the point. But, if the multicolored garment was indeed the principal cause of the entire Egyptian exile, why not actually bring a multicolored garment to the Seder table and mention it candidly, in order to ensure that no one will miss this crucial information? Is it not vital to know what caused the bondage in Egypt, before we tell the story of how and when the Israelites were freed? What is the purpose of making the Seder participants aware of this only on a subconscious level, instead of bringing it to the surface?

I believe that this touches on the very core of Judaism's interpretation of the Exodus. Its main point is to emphasize Divine providence, God's miraculous interference in the lives of millions of Jews who were stranded and enslaved in Egypt. This story had to become the *locus classicus* of all Jewish history. Whatever happens is ultimately in God's hands. This is the categorical lesson of the Pesach story. It is not the story of the human role in history, or to what extent human beings had a hand in shaping all of the events that took place. Of course, Jewish tradition constantly emphasizes that one has to take responsibility for the consequences of his deeds, but the Pesach story operates on a different level. It is the triumph of God as the Lord of History that is celebrated.

In fact, the interplay between Divine intervention and human action is one of the great philosophical problems, which all religious thinkers have grappled with. To what extent are we responsible, and to what extent is God responsible? This question remains basically unanswered and is part of the mystery of human history.

This also touches on another unsolvable problem. How can we ever know what is the cause that brings about a specific effect?

More than that, when is something actually a cause and not the effect of an earlier incident?

Regarding the Egyptian enslavement, are we indeed able to say for sure that it was just the hatred of the brothers for Yosef that brought about the Jews' servitude, and if the brothers had not sold Yosef to Egypt, the Israelites would not have landed in Egypt? Wasn't it promised to Avraham that his children would be enslaved in a land that was not theirs?[5] The Egyptian experience is seen in its own right as a *sine qua non* to prepare the Jews for receiving the Torah and shaping them into a spiritual people that will be a "light unto the nations." So to what extent were the brothers really responsible for this exile, and how much free will did they actually exercise when they decided to sell their brother?

It is for these reasons that the authors of the Haggada were not prepared to openly point their finger at the brothers. They could do nothing but allude to this fact, telling us that somewhere along the road to Egypt the *"karpas* garment" dipped in blood played a role. We may never know to what extent, but it is most telling that the *karpas* is eaten at the very beginning of the Haggada reading. It makes us immediately aware that the inside story of what really caused the exile in Egypt will remain forever a mystery. That is the all-encompassing, underlying message that this ritual wants to convey at the very beginning, before we continue to read the story. It will indeed provoke many questions. But however brilliant the answers, we will be left with the knowledge that on a higher plane, and beyond human understanding, it is the hand of God that holds the answers.

On a moral level, however, the story should be clear. It was hatred between brothers that sent us into exile. It is revealing that what brought about the redemption was the love between two brothers, Moshe and Aaron, living in total harmony.

---

5. *Bereshit* 15:13.

Questions to Ponder
from the DCA Think Tank

1. Understanding the word "karpas" as "fine woolen fabric" is based on the description of the king's banquet hall in Esther 1:6. Therefore, the karpas ritual might also be hinting at that story, which has many parallels to the Yosef story. How are Yosef and Esther similar? How are they different? What might we learn from the comparison?

2. The author states, "Had Yaakov not given the garment to Yosef, the exile and servitude in Egypt would in all likelihood not have come about." Assuming that the descent to Egypt and servitude there were an essential part of the Divine plan, could not that end have been accomplished by other means? If not, how can the brothers be held morally responsible for playing their assigned role in the drama?

3. Rabbi Cardozo writes: "The Egyptian experience is seen in its own right as a sine qua non to prepare the Jews for receiving the Torah and shaping them into a spiritual people that will be a 'light unto the nations'." If this is the case, is there any significance to exactly what set that experience in motion, especially since the slavery itself came only in the next generation?

Freedom of Will and Determinism: A Daring Midrash

ויוסף הורד מצרימה

And Yosef was brought down to Egypt. *Bereshit 39:1*

"WE MUST BELIEVE in freedom of will; we have no choice." This observation by Isaac Bashevis Singer introduces one of the greatest problems in Jewish and secular philosophy — the dilemma of freedom of will versus determinism. Many have attempted to resolve the issue, but not one philosopher has been able to come up with a completely satisfactory response.

In *Midrash Tanchuma*,[1] we come across one of the most daring statements ever made in religious literature. It is a telling example of the boldness of our sages, who were not afraid to deal with the problem of free will "head on."

On the words "And Yosef was brought down to Egypt,"[2] the midrash comments: "This is what is referred to when it says: 'Come and see the works of God. He is terrible in His dealing (*alila*) with men.'"[3]

---

1. *Midrash Tanchuma*, Warsaw ed., Vayeshev 4.
2. Bereshit 39:1.
3. Tehillim 66:5.

Alila — God's false accusation

The expression *"alila"* is open to many interpretations and is unclear. Still, on the surface, the verse in which the word appears seems to express a principal Jewish belief that teaches us about the greatness of God. Viewed in this light, the translation of *"alila"* seems to convey the concept of awesomeness. However, it is clear that the midrash realizes that the expression, *"alila,"* is in fact most unconventional, for it continues with the following words:

> Says Rabbi Yehoshua ben Korcha, "Even those events which You [God] bring upon us, You bring with *'alila.'* Before God created the world, He created the Angel of Death on the first day." From where do we know this? Said Rabbi Barchiah, "Because it is written [when the creation had just begun]: 'there was darkness upon the face of the deep.'[4] This is a reference to the Angel of Death who darkens the face of all creatures. Adam was created on the sixth day and an *'alila'* was placed before him so that he would bring death upon the world, as it is written, 'And on the day that you will eat from it [i.e., the Tree of Knowledge] you will surely die.(Bereshit 2:17)"[5]

This means that *from the outset* it was determined that Adam and Hava would be *forced* to eat from the tree, because they *had* to be mortal, since God had already created the necessity for death.

It now becomes clear that the word *"alila"* means according to the midrash *false accusation*, *pretext* or *insidiousness*. Yet, according to the plain text of the Torah, death came upon Mankind because humans *chose* to eat from the tree.

In case we question the correctness of this interpretation, let us read the continuation of this midrash in which the following analogy is brought:

---
4. Bereshit 1:2.
5. Ibid., 2:17.

To what can we compare this case? To a man who wished to divorce his wife. Before he went home, he wrote a *"get"* (bill of divorce) and entered the house with the *get* in his pocket. He then sought an *"alila"* to give it to her. He told her, "Pour me a cup that I may drink." She poured it for him. When he took the cup from her, he said, "Here is your *'get.'*" She said to him, "What did I do wrong?" He said, "Go out of my house because you poured for me a lukewarm cup." Said she to him, "Did you already know that I would pour for you a lukewarm cup, so that you wrote a *get* and brought it in your hand?" So Adam said to the Holy One blessed be He, "Lord of the universe, before You created the world, the Torah was with You for 2,000 years [i.e., eternally]. You wrote in the Torah about 'a man who dies in a tent,'[6] and now you come to accuse me that *I* brought death to the world?!"[7]

The Waters of Meriva

The midrash continues in a similar vein, recounting the story of Moshe and the waters of *"meriva"* (the episode in which Moshe sinned by hitting the rock instead of speaking to it as God had instructed him to do in order to bring forth water for the people of Israel.[8] The midrash proves from the text that this sin was already determined long before Moshe erred in this way, and still he was blamed for having brought about his own downfall due to this "transgression."

The third example brought by the midrash relates to our parashah — Yosef and the exile in Egypt. In *Bereshit* we read that Avraham is told by God, "Know for sure that your descendants will be aliens in a land which is not theirs, and will be slaves

---

6. *Bamidbar* 19:14.
7. Midrash Tanchuma, Warsaw ed., Vayeshev 4.
8. *Bamidbar* 20.

and oppressed for four hundred years."⁹ Says the midrash: God blamed the entire affair — the jealousy and the hatred between the brothers and Yosef, the sale of Yosef, his elevation to high office in Egypt and ultimately the coming of Yaakov and his sons to Egypt — on all of them in order to fulfill what He had said to Avraham.

In other words: the brothers are blamed for having caused all this to happen when, in actual fact, the whole outcome was already decided in advance! Therefore, it is an *"alila"*!

Those who study this narrative very carefully will realize, however, that the midrash was not forced to give this interpretation. It could have allowed for an explanation which would lean towards freedom of will. Therefore we must conclude that it *deliberately* took this route to emphasize the paradox of freedom of will versus determinism, and to teach us an important lesson. When Jews declare, "*Hakol biyadey shamaim chutz meyirat shamaim* — everything is from Heaven [determinism] except the fear of Heaven [freedom of will],"¹⁰ they pronounce a profound tenet of Jewish belief. It is not that there are certain times when determinism operates, and other times when humans have free will. Rather, both principles function simultaneously: on one level, human beings seem to have the ability to choose; however, on a different level, all is predetermined. This is one of the great paradoxes of human existence. It reminds us of an observation by Friedrich Dürrenmatt, who once said that "he who confronts himself with the paradoxical, exposes himself to reality."¹¹

---

9. *Bereshit* 15:13.
10. *Berachot* 33a.
11. Friedrich Dürrenmatt, *Plays and Essays* (New York: Continuum, 1982), 156.

Questions to Ponder
from the DCA Think Tank

1. In your personal life, do you feel you have complete freedom of will in your decisions or do you feel its all part of a larger divine plan (or perhaps, in the spirit of this essay, do you feel both simultaneously?)

2. How do you feel about the concept of God as carrying out an alila — as understood by the Midrash to mean a plot, false accusations, pretense or insidiousness? Does this notion undermine your faith in Divine providence?

3. How do you, personally, reconcile the paradox between divine oversight of history and human free will? Does the paradox make you uncomfortable? If so, what is the source of this discomfort?

Divine Emanations and Human Responses

ויהי מקץ שנתים ימים ופרעה חלם

It came to pass at the end of two years that
Pharaoh dreamed a dream... *Bereshit 41:1*

HISTORY, THE STUDY of cause and effect in the annals of humankind, has been a serious challenge for honest historians. In many ways, interpreting history is conjecture. What motivates many a historian is more what one would *like* to believe happened than what *actually* occurred. After all, how can any historian ever really differentiate cause from effect in a specific instance? Sometimes, what we believe to be the cause is actually the effect.

Our sages draw our attention to this phenomenon when they deal with the sale of Yosef and his emancipation from prison. Referring to the words, "A definite period was set for the world to spend in darkness",[1] the Midrash states: "A definite number of years was fixed for Joseph to spend in prison, in darkness. When the appointed time came: "It came to pass at the end of two years that Pharaoh dreamed a dream...""[2]

Rabbi Gedalyah Schorr, in his monumental work, *Ohr Gedalyah*, points out that this observation radically differs from the traditional, academic way of dealing with historical events.

---

1. Iyov 28:3
2. Bereshit 41:1, Midrash Rabbah

Reading the story in the traditional way, we would no doubt conclude that *because* Pharaoh dreamed a dream which required an interpretation, Joseph, known to be a man with prophetic insights into dream interpretation, was asked to come and see Pharaoh. After having successfully solved the dreams, he was not only freed but elevated to the position of second-in-command of Egypt. This would mean that Pharaoh's dream *caused* Joseph's freedom.

A careful reading of our Midrash, however, suggests the reverse. It was because Joseph *had* to be freed and become the viceroy of Egypt that Pharaoh *had* to have a dream. The cause was, in fact, the effect.

Judaism suggests that at certain times God sends emanations to this world so as to awaken human beings to act, just as Pharaoh received his dreams in order that Joseph's imprisonment would come to an end.

The Maccabees: the needs of the hour

A later example of this is the story of Hanukkah. The Jews knew that logically there was no chance of a successful uprising against the Greeks, but God created a notion of revolt within the minds of the Maccabees. The greatness of these few Jews was manifest in their correct reaction to this heavenly directive. They realized what needed to be done, however preposterous.

Midrashic literature[3] often compares the Greek empire to "darkness which blinded the eyes of the Jews" ("*Hoshech ze Yavan*", "Darkness is Greece"). The traditional interpretation is that Jews in the Maccabean period were blinded by the Greeks' worship of the body and followed their example.

It may, however, have a much deeper meaning. The Greeks were also the inventors of historical interpretation. Greek thinkers were among the first to try and understand history in its more scientific

---

3. Bereshit Rabba, Vilna ed., Vilna Ed., 2:4.

form as reflected in the need to search for cause and effect. From the point of view of the Midrash, this approach blinded the Jews from sometimes reading history as divine emanations and the human response to them. It misconstrued the deeper meaning of history, reversing cause and effect, and *darkened* the clear insight of the Jews.

The Mystery of Changing Tastes

One of the most mysterious aspects of the human psyche is the dimension of motivation and taste. We suddenly hear an inner voice or feel a mysterious pull to do something, the source of which we do not understand. This is true not only of human actions but even taste and preference. History is replete with examples of human beings radically changing their taste in art and music. Melodies are considered to be superb and irreplaceable; then, half a century later, they lose favor. So it is with art, fashion and even the color of our wallpaper.

There are no rational explanations for these phenomena (notwithstanding various scientific suggestions). We would argue that these are the result of divine emanations communicated to our world. While it is difficult to explain *why* these divine messages come, perhaps their main purpose, particularly regarding music and art, is to offer us a feeling of renewal and an insight into the infinite possibilities of God's creation. Some messages may be a divine response to our earlier deeds or moral condition. The sudden predilections for more aggressive forms of music or art *may* be a warning that we have strayed from our earlier dignity.

Hearing the Divine

The main challenge is in "hearing" the message, correctly interpreting it and subsequently knowing what it demands of us. This itself requires divine assistance and moral integrity, and is not available to all. (In fact, it can be dangerous.)

Throughout history, Jews have experienced many divine emanations. Several of them, cited in the latter part of Tanach, allude to the coming of the Mashiach at specific times. (See, for example, the book of Daniel.) Some of these dates are long behind us and Mashiach has not appeared. This should not surprise us. Dates of Mashiach's arrival, as cited in Jewish sources, were in no way final statements. They were divine signals that at these times the world would be more conducive to the coming of Mashiach, but they were not *guarantees* of his arrival. When humankind failed to respond in the appropriate religious and moral manner, the special moment passed with no outcome.

It is easy to recognize in this day and age that we too are confronted with new and powerful happenings which may be emanations from above. One cannot deny the unique events which have transpired in Israel over the last seventy years. Many of them — the good events as well as the dire ones — are difficult to explain by the conventional standards of historical interpretation. It behooves us to view much what is happening today in Israel as a divine message that there is need for a radical change of heart regarding our identity, our Jewish connection, the moral quality of our society, and Judaism at large. It may be worthwhile to contemplate this possibility and act accordingly.

Questions to Ponder
from the DCA Think Tank

1. Do you agree with the basic premise of this essay that "Sometimes, what we believe to be the cause is actually the effect"? Can you think of historical situations that might be explained on this basis? What about in your personal life?

2. Do you agree with the author that there are no rational explanations for things like art, music, and fashion? What "divine message" might such phenomena be sending us?

3. Rabbi Cardozo states that the main challenge is "hearing" the divine message. What might stand in the way of our "hearing" such a message? Do you feel that it's ever safe to act on a presumption that we have "heard" the divine message? Under what circumstances would you be willing to trust such a message?

4. Do you see the re-establishment of the Jewish state to be as the result of a divine emanation? Do you feel that there is a divine message in this and in Israel's subsequent blossoming? If so, what sort of "human response" is called for in the face of such a divine message?

The Tragedy of the Tzaddik

> ויוסף הוא השליט על הארץ הוא
> המשביר לכל עם הארץ...
>
> Now Yosef was the ruler over the land;
> it was he who sold grain to the entire
> populace of the land. *Bereshit 42:6*

IT IS REMARKABLE that of the Avot, the three forefathers of the People of Israel, not one of them was officially called a tzaddik (righteous man) by the Talmudic and midrashic Sages. Only Yaakov's son Yosef was granted that title.[1] This is rather strange, since it cannot be denied that Avraham, Yitzhak and Yaakov were also outstandingly pious people.

It may be that the reason for this special honor is because, paradoxically, Yosef did not at all appear to be a tzaddik. If anything, the reverse might have been more accurate.

There can be little doubt that during Yosef's reign in Egypt, he must have been seen as a ruthless person who didn't hesitate to make the lives of his fellow people unbearable, particularly those of his brothers and father. We should not overlook the fact that the Torah and commentaries offer readers a huge advantage, telling them the whole story in just a few chapters, so they have no time to resent Yosef before discovering his righteousness at the end of

---

1. See *Midrash Tanchuma*, Buber ed., *Noah* 4.

the story! This privilege, however, was not granted to any of the people with whom Yosef actually spent a good part of his life.

Yosef's life is the epitome of complicated human existence in the extreme. It is a life in which human conditions are far from ideal. There are no black-and-white choices, where it is easy to take a stand, and where the good guys and bad guys are clearly identified. Every choice includes a complex mixture of good and bad. Even with the best intentions, people sometimes cannot help hurting those they love the most, and doing favors for those who are corrupt.

Population transfer

Reading the story, one wonders what must have gone through Yosef's mind and heart when he took a tough stand against the people of Egypt. He bought up everything they owned, leaving the entire population with no personal possessions, and enslaved to Pharaoh. The text also clearly indicates that Yosef uprooted everyone from their homes; and all of them became refugees in their own country.[2] This was nothing less than mass population transfer and dispersal, one of the worst human experiences. Commentators explain that this was the only way he was able to save the country from even greater disaster and, in fact, the only way to revive the economy.[3] Still, it must have greatly distressed him to bring about such upheaval in the nation. Few could have understood what he did, and millions must have cursed him for making their lives miserable.

Yosef's behavior toward his father and brothers also must have caused him sleepless nights, year after year. While ruling the Land of Egypt, he never told his father that he was still alive. His

---

2. Bereshit 47.
3. See Sigmund A. Wagner-Tsukamoto, "The Genesis of Economic Cooperation in the Stories of Joseph: A Constitutional and Institutional Economic Reconstruction," *Scandinavian Journal of the Old Testament* 29, no. 1 (2015): 33-54.

own life must have been unbearable every time he thought of his suffering father. *How can I endure one more day knowing that my father is in constant anguish because of me?*

His terribly strong stand against his brothers, when they came to Egypt to buy food, must have given him nightmares and caused him depression as well. *What will my brothers and all the servants in the palace think of me? In their eyes I must seem like a cruel despot looking for sadistic ways to hurt people whenever possible. What are they thinking of me as I am imprisoning Shimon and forcing my brothers to bring Binyamin to Egypt?*

Revealing true motivation?

Still, as many commentators explain, Yosef had no option but to do what he did. In fact, it was his deep devotion and his concern for those he loved that motivated him.[4] Surely he must have dreamed of the day when he would be able to reveal to those he had hurt the true motivation behind his harsh actions.

But, as the Torah clearly reveals, even *this* Yosef was not granted. His father never knew what his real motives were, and his brothers clearly showed after the death of their father that they suspected Yosef would take revenge on them.[5] How painful it must have been for Yosef to realize that even in his old age he could not tell anybody why he had acted as he did without revealing what his brothers had in fact done to him. And that was not an option for him.

He was convinced that he would go to his grave considered by millions to have been a merciless leader. The fact that he had saved the Egyptian economy would make little difference in the eyes of all who would never comprehend why he needed to achieve

---

4. See, for example, the commentaries of Ramban and Rabbi Samson Raphael Hirsch on this Chapter.
5. *Bereshit* 50:15.

that goal through the harsh measures he took. Their expression of gratitude[6] may well have been the kind of forced courtesy often given to a dictator.

What a relief it would have been for him to know that hundreds of years later, the Torah and its commentators would reveal the entire story and prove his righteous intentions! Still, one wonders whether he would have even agreed that God include this story in the Torah, giving his brothers a bad name!

The utter conviction of the tzaddik

This, indeed, is the tragedy of practically every tzaddik. Tzaddikim are, for the most part, people who are unable to reveal their true intentions and righteousness. Often they must work under the most agonizing circumstances, sometimes hurting people when it is the only way to prevent an even greater tragedy. This is the reason why they cannot always be "nice guys" and "well-mannered people."

Tzaddikim hold to a higher purpose; they cannot allow themselves to sway with the winds. The saying "When you stand for nothing you fall for everything" applies to them. But standing for something may very well give one a bad name, no matter how noble the intentions. The tzaddik can only hope that perhaps someday, people will discover what they were really all about and how painful it was to be a "hidden tzaddik." Unfortunately, there is usually little chance of that happening. After all, who is as privileged as Yosef to have his or her *real* story written in an eternal book?

This is the reason why the title "tzaddik" was bestowed upon Yosef in particular. While it is true that his father, grandfather and great-grandfather were illustrious people, the sages realized that only Yosef had to do so much that he detested doing, so as to

---

6. Ibid., 47:25.

become a real tzaddik. In fact, the Midrash makes it abundantly clear that it was the tough measures he took that earned him the title "tzaddik."

To be righteous, with the full awareness that nobody will ever know the real story, and to have one's deeds condemned, is one of the most painful human experiences and is a great tragedy. Only the knowledge that the One Above knows the real story, as well as the conviction that it is more important that others benefit from one's deeds than to be assured of the recognition of one's real intentions — only this gives the ultimate feeling of spiritual satisfaction for which the tzaddik strives.

Questions to Ponder
from the DCA Think Tank

1. Rabbi Cardozo writes, "It may, however, be suggested that the reason for this special honor is because, paradoxically, Yosef did not at all appear to be a real tzaddik. If anything, the reverse." Noah, too, was explicitly called a tzaddik, despite his later odd behavior. And, though no woman is called tzaddika in Tanach, Yehudah points out that Tamar *"tzadka mimeni"*—admitting that she was more "tzaddika" or righteous than he. This, though Tamar, too, did not seem much like a tzaddika—in fact, she posed as a prostitute!

   Notwithstanding the above, nowadays the term "tzaddik" or "tzaddeket" almost always makes people think of people who pray and learn all day and never sin, rather than the complex characters Rabbi Cardozo describes. Why have we abandoned the original concept?

2. Rabbi Cardozo writes that when one knows Yosef's full story, one cannot bear a grudge against him. But once we know someone's whole story, is it *ever* possible to bear a grudge against them? Could anyone ever be judged as wicked if we could theoretically trace his/her actions and motivations from their origins? What is your opinion?

3. If you believe we cannot separate individual actions from their context in order to judge them, what does this say about free choice? And if we *can* separate individual actions from their context in order to judge them, then what exempts Joseph from being called ruthless?

4. Joshua Sobol wrote the excellent play *Ghetto* about the Vilna Ghetto. The play features Jacob Gens, based on the real man who headed the ghetto, who made deep compromises and worked with the German authorities in order to save Jews. Gens is still seen by some as a collaborator and by some as a pragmatic hero. Do you think Gens was a modern-day Yosef? Do you think that those who see him as a wicked man would continue to do so if they could see his whole story?

5. Why can't a tzaddik sway with the winds? What is the line between "swaying with the winds" and allowing oneself to consider the new information and changing values of society? Must one be hermetically sealed, or intransigent, in order to be a true tzaddik? And does not this contradict Rabbi Cardozo's suggestion that a tzaddik is a complex person?

6. Could the tzaddik/a be representative of a group within the Jewish people, one that, for example, does not allow itself to sway with the winds? Are there other equally important Jewish archetypes that are representative of other groups within the nation? e.g. the *rahman/a, amcha, navi/nevi'a, The chacham/a, hassid/a, nazir/nezira* or *kanai/t* (merciful person,

Miketz

ordinary citizen, prophet, wise/learned person, mystical, devoted person, ascetic, zealot)?

What other types could you think of? Which of these most describes you or the group with which you identify?

Vayigash

Generational Awareness

> ויגש אליו יהודה ויאמר בי אדני ידבר
> נא עבדך דבר באזני אדני ואל יחר אפך
> בעבדך כי כמוך כפרעה אדני שאל את
> עבדיו לאמר היש לכם אב או אח
>
> Then Yehuda went up to him and said, "Please, my lord, let your servant appeal to my lord, and do not be impatient with your servant, you who are the equal of Pharaoh. My lord asked his servants, 'Have you a father or another brother?'" *Bereshit 44:18*

THE JEWISH PEOPLE'S relationship with time is paradoxical and complex. We are a people with a long history and great hopes for the future. We still experience the exodus of Egypt as if it were happening today. At the same time, we enjoy a blissful glimpse of Olam Haba (the world to come) every Shabbat as we sit at our Shabbat tables like kings and queens; our enchanted dreams of the future become momentarily realized.

However, despite our glorious past and marvelous vision of the future, we have difficulty relating to the "here and now." As Jews, we do not feel at ease within the limited confines of the "present." We are in need of a "space" in which we can include the past and the future and condense them into the present. This is far from easy. What we need is what Rabbi Joseph B. Soloveitchik calls:

"Generation Awareness."

Rabbi Soloveitchik relates an unforgettable lesson that he learned from his *melamed* (teacher) when he was a young boy studying in *heder*.[1] The boys were learning the biblical story of Yosef and his brothers. The Torah relates how Yosef questioned his brothers "Have you a father, or a brother?" to which his brothers replied: "We have an old father and a young child of his old age…" (Bereshit 44:19).

But why ask the question in this way? Yosef, the *melamed* concluded, was anxious to know whether his brothers felt themselves committed to their roots, to their origins. Were they "origin conscious"? Are you, Yosef asked the brothers, rooted in your father? Do you look upon him the way the branches, or the blossoms, look upon the roots of the tree? Do you look upon your father as the feeder, as the foundation of your existence? Do you look upon him as the provider and sustainer of your existence? Or are you a band of rootless shepherds who forgot their origin, who wander from place to place, from pasture to pasture?

"*Ha-yesh lachem av?* Do you have a father?" the melamed said, means: Are you proud of your fathers? Of what they stand for? If you do, if you admit to the supremacy of your own fathers and ancestors, then, *ipso facto*, you admit to the supremacy of the Universal Father, the ancient Creator of the world who is called *Atik Yomim* ("Ancient of Days").

This is generation awareness.

We find this concept of generation awareness in connection with the Sinai revelation:

"I make this covenant and this oath not with you alone but with those who are here standing with us this day before the Lord your God and those who are not with us today." (Devarim 29:13-14).

Rashi comments that "those who are not with us today" means

---

[1]. "Do You Have a Father?" Rabbi Joseph B. Soloveitchik, http://www.chabad.org/library/article_cdo/aid/3221/jewish/Do-You-Have-a-Father.htm

all the future generations.

What does this mean?

It means that Jews do not live *in* time; they *transcend* time. We are a nation that transcends history and is lifted into eternity.

All Jews stood at Sinai, even those who were not physically present. Similarly, the Talmud[2] relates an "encounter" between Moshe Rabenu and Rabbi Akiva even though, historically speaking, they could never have met!

In our study halls, Maimonides could have a discussion with the Gaon of Vilna, and the Baal Shem Tov can sit in the Tent of Avraham Avinu and discuss the halachic observations made by the Talmudic sages. Wherever and whenever Jews live, they live in "eternal time" and they all meet in the same Beit Midrash.

Over the thousands of years of exile we maintained a connection wherever we found ourselves. We kept discussing our mission and debating the Talmud, even though we lived thousands of miles apart and hundreds of years removed. We are the first "Internet" people and were able to enter a "time machine" and get out in every century we wanted. This made us into a nation which by its very definition could never fit into community of nations.

Getting lost in the river of time

In our age, there is little sense of historical continuity. Things move at such a quick pace that we lose the ability to keep track of time. Thus we enter into a state of time-detachment and a-temporality. We can compare this mindset to what is known in the philosophy of science as a paradigm shift, i.e. a scientific development that is not the product of a gradual and incremental improvement upon earlier scientific discoveries, but a completely new discovery. Such a thing is totally unprecedented and "hits" us unexpectedly with

---

2. Menahot, 29b

utter amazement.

In science, this is a great triumph. But in everyday life, it may have deleterious psychological side-effects. When we lose our connection with the "before" — when memories of the past are no longer important — we lose our road map to the future. We need to be rooted in the past in order to leap toward the future.

As Jews, we are highly aware of the dangers of this. We know that if there is anything that keeps us alive it is the eternal bond between the generations. As a nation small in numbers, we know that we cannot survive by might alone. There can be no future if there is no continuity with the past.

More than any other nation, we depend on a strong attachment to our past. We have no numbers to count on. If we forget our generation awareness we will, just like many other nations, disintegrate rapidly. This is beside the fact that any desire to be a nation like all the others will be undermined by a world which does not want us to "be counted among the nations." This is clearly demonstrated by the great animosity that Israel has to deal with.

Today we realize that we have too much history, too little geography, too many hopes for the future, and too few members to survive. We survive only by a miracle. Therefore we need to create a strong bond between our fellow Jews and their ancestors in order to create a brighter future. It is time for us to wake up and find our way back to what our forefathers stood for.

The ties that bind

Our children and our grandchildren hold for us great hopes and dreams. We hope that they will speak our language, think our thoughts, feel our sentiments, and hold onto our priorities. We hope they will implement our vision and cherish our ideals. We want them to belong to the "fraternity of the committed." If this happens, we are confident that there will be a future.

But what are the essential components that constitute the

"fraternity of the committed"? Is it just halachic living? Is it the uncompromising commitment to the code of Jewish law which forms this bond?

The answer is clearly in the negative. Halachic observance alone cannot create this kind of fraternity. We are in need of something more in order to move Judaism forward as a spiritually vital and existentially meaningful experience. This essential ingredient is something that seemingly many religious Jews today have forgotten.

The Talmud asks the question how it is possible that we recite a bracha (blessing) before we light the hannukiah which includes the praise of God: "Who has *commanded* us to kindle the lights of Hanukkah."[3] But where is it stated in the Torah that we need to light candles on Hanukkah? After all, this is a Rabbinic institution. There is no mention of this in the Torah, since the story of Hanukkah took place hundreds of years after the giving of the Torah.

The Talmud gives us two answers:

Rav Avya said (that the justification for this bracha which states that we are commanded to light the candles) is *"You shall not deviate from the word they (the sages) will tell you"* (Devarim 17:11). This means that since God commanded us to listen to whatever the sages pronounced as Halacha, it is as if God Himself has commanded us to do so, therefore we can say: "Who commanded us."

Rav Nehemiah offered an alternative solution and said that the source for this ruling is: *"Ask you father and he will tell you and your elders and they will say to you"* (Devarim 32:7).

The Netziv, Rabbi Natftali Tzvi Yehudah Berlin, the head of the famous Volozhin Yeshiva, (19th century) emphasizes that the statement of Rav Nehemiah teaches us about the power of

---

3. Shabbat 23a

custom, not Halacha. The "father and elders" in the verse in Devarim 32:7 is not referring to the sages of Israel, but to our *own personal* ancestors who initiated certain practices which later became customs and traditions in our families. In only a few instances were these traditions later established as Halacha, such as in the case of lighting the candles on Hanukkah. It started as a custom and was slowly adopted by the people of Israel and eventually became law. Ultimately it was felt as if God Himself had commanded us to light the candles.

But most of the time, the meaning of the phrase "Ask your father and he will tell you, and your elders, and they will say to you" does not refer to Halacha but the need to adopt family traditions and customs.

This is a most important and unusual observation. The Netziv introduces us to the power of Jewish customs *(minhag), as distinct from Halacha*. These traditions shape the unique character of individual families and communities. They are extremely powerful in binding families and communities together in ways that Halacha cannot achieve.

Halacha applies to all; it is not able to create specific customs which belong to one family and not to another. In this sense Halacha fails to create the kind of *particularistic* bond which is crucial to the continuation of Jewish life. There is a strong need for exclusiveness and *individuality* of Jewish families and communities in order to ensure that Jews *as a nation* continue to survive and flourish.

This is the power of custom. But custom is much more than a specific set of family *practices*. It also involves certain familial expressions, songs, foods, and even body language. Halacha teaches us how to act, but it cannot provide insight into the quality of the act. It provides the musical score, but it is not the performance of the music itself. *Minhag* is the corrective to this. It is flexible and adds color and warmth to our family life. It generates a distinctive ambiance and creates the culture of specific families and communities. It has no halachic rules and thus it is able to provide us with a *living* bond between family members and communities. It is responsible for the feeling which families are so much in need of, namely, uniqueness and exclusiveness.

Once we have connected with the past as individuals, we can easily introduce ourselves into the future. We will even be able to meet our future relatives. They may not have been born yet, but they are already part of our family. We already know who they are, how they will live their Jewish lives, what values they will adhere to, and what life choices they will make. Together with the past generations, we will meet them in our present.

This is the meaning of "generation awareness." Jewish survival depends on the conscious link between earlier and later generations. Rabbi Solovietchik calls this the "mesora community," a community in which traditions and customs are passed down from generation to generation, not as ancient customs and quaint relics of the past but as living experiences in which we take enormous pride. Thus, Yosef's question to his brothers had an answer: "Yes, we have a father!"

Questions to Ponder
from the DCA Think Tank

1. "Jews do not live in time; they transcend time. We are a nation that transcends history and is lifted into eternity." What Rabbi Cardozo calls "generation awareness" is therefore, in one sense, the opposite of historical awareness. With generation awareness, Maimonides, the Vilna Gaon and the Baal Shem Tov all meet in the same Beit Midrash. Historical

awareness, by contrast, invites us to ask what Talmudic legal discussions or Maimonidean philosophical writings meant in their particular historical context and therefore to think about how we should apply those texts in our contemporary world.

Is there a place for this kind of "historical awareness" alongside Judaism's "generation awareness"; in other words, to see ourselves as living in time as well as transcending time?

2. "We need to be rooted in the past in order to leap toward the future." As Rabbi Cardozo explains it, to be rooted in the past means to have pride in one's ancestors and in what they stood for. Rootedness, in other words, is a mixture of group (or kinship) identity and religious or moral values. How do these two things work together to create a sense of rootedness?

3. Rabbi Cardozo contrasts the sense of historical continuity with the procedures of science. Science is only interested in discovering the truth about the world. If an earlier scientific theory turns out to be wrong, science has no further use for it. Is there any place for this kind of critical thinking in the Jewish tradition or are science and religion mutually exclusive realms? If critique of the past is possible within religion, what forms does it take? And how is it compatible with the sense of historical continuity?

4. Rabbi Cardozo argues that custom (minhag) has a crucial role to play alongside Halacha in maintaining the continuity of Jewish life. In order to ensure the continuity of the Jewish nation as a whole we also need the particularistic bonds that tie individual families and communities together from generation to generation.

How true is this of your own connection to Judaism? Do

childhood memories of particular family or community traditions, for example, form an important part of your Jewish identity? If so, what are these memories — Pesach Seder, sitting in the sukkah, synagogue melodies from the High Holy Days, songs and stories you heard from your parents and grandparents? Are there traditions that you cherish from your past and that you seek to transmit to your children thereby creating a bond between Jewish part and Jewish future?

Do you think there is a place creating new (family and community) traditions in Judaism, or is this a contradiction in terms?

Do you agree with Rabbi Cardozo's claim that the Jewish nation will only survive and flourish if it leaves space for individualistic and particularistic expression? In your experience, how successful is the Jewish community in making space for, and encouraging, such individualistic expression? What do you think are the proper limits on such particularistic expression?

Arguing Against Oneself: Yosef's Revenge

ועתה אל תעצבו ואל יחר בעיניכם כי מכרתם
אתי הנה כי למחיה שלחני אלהים לפניכם

But now do not be sad, and let it not trouble
you that you sold me here, for it was to preserve
life that God sent me before you. *Bereshit 45:5*

FEW THINGS ARE as difficult as taking revenge while remaining righteous. The combination seems paradoxical. Even harder, though, is *not* to take revenge. It is sometimes inconceivable. An injustice enters the innermost chambers of the victim's heart, festering and tenacious. Its devastating effect can destroy the victim's life as few things can. It cries for an outlet in vengeance.

How does one master one's desire for retaliation and not be destroyed by it? Is it possible *not* to bear a grudge? Feelings of revenge cannot be eliminated simply by denying them. They will surely explode, and the aftermath will be even worse than the original revenge one would have liked to take but suppressed.

Taking revenge vs. bearing a grudge

How, then, can the Torah forbid any form of retaliation? "You shall neither take revenge nor bear a grudge against the members of your people."[1] Is this not asking the impossible? Is it not, in fact, dangerous? We might understand that one is not allowed to take revenge in the form of *action*, but not even to bear a grudge seems to be impossible, as well as counterproductive. One cannot suppress feelings without expecting consequences.

How did Yosef deal with his feelings of injustice after his brothers mistreated him and sold him into slavery? Did he *really* not take revenge or bear a grudge against them, as many commentators claim? Even the biblical text seems to present this as a possibility when it tells us how Yosef's brothers were worried that he would hold their treatment of him against them after their father Yaakov died:

> Yosef's brothers saw that their father had died, and they said: Perhaps Yosef will hate us, and will pay us back for all the evil that we did to him.[2]

> And Yosef said to them: Fear not, for am I in the place of God? Though you intended evil against me, God designed it for the good, to make the outcome as it actually is on this day, to keep a great nation alive.[3]

Why, then, did Yosef not reveal himself at the first opportunity that arose, when his brothers stood before him? Instead, he teases them mercilessly. He bids them to come and then sends them away; arrests them after he has money and his royal cup planted in one brother's sack; throws one of them into jail, and puts them all in a state of mortal fear. If this is not revenge, what is? Commentators struggle with this episode and have come up with explanations, some of them brilliant, and some weak.

Yosef is a skillful psychologist. His self-perception is supreme.

---

1. *Vayikra* 19:18.
2. *Bereshit* 50:15.
3. *Ibid.* 19-20.

He realizes that revenge is a futile attempt to remedy past suffering. Vengeance cannot be defended as "teaching the aggressor a lesson," or "getting even." It simply doesn't work. Rather than bringing closure after suffering violence and injury, revenge spirals and escalates. But one cannot take a moral stand based on suppressing the urge toward revenge. This also will not work; for it would require humans to be angels.

Instead, the rage that feeds vengeance should be redirected to positive thought and action. The impulse toward revenge must be weakened; in its place, genuine sorrow should emerge. The need for retaliation must be given time to slowly die out. It cannot be killed overnight.

"Vengeful healing"

At the same time, it is necessary to cause the perpetrator to realize his mistake, make peace with himself and sincerely repent. Revenge can be meaningful only if it is healing to both the victim and the perpetrator. Then, it is no longer vengeance but "vengeful healing". What Yosef does is to set up a strategy by which both conditions are fulfilled.

Yosef does not take actual revenge. All he does is allow his subconscious to have its way and believe that he *is* taking revenge. While his reason dictates not to retaliate, because it has no purpose, he knows that feelings of hate may be lurking in his subconscious even as he is unaware of them. His experience with dreams, via the baker, the wine butler, and Pharaoh, has taught him how powerful is the subliminal voice. There is no escape, however much one would like to remove any feelings of vengeance. It *must* get its way. Otherwise, it may manifest itself in the most forceful manner and cause enormous damage. To ignore it is a major mistake. It needs to be acknowledged. There must be revenge, even if it goes against one's better judgment. But it should never manifest itself in deeds; it can only be subconscious revenge.

Yosef is aware of yet another aspect of the need for retaliation. It is necessary for the perpetrators to think that he *had* his revenge, after which, there can be complete closure.

Tricking the Subconscious

Thus, what Yosef does is most ingenious. He tricks his subconscious as well as his brothers by creating a strategy that makes all parties believe that he actually is taking revenge. In this way, he satisfies all sides.

At the same time, he must make sure that his brothers have the opportunity to repent for their mistakes, and that can be done only if he creates a scenario where they find themselves in a similar situation as at the time when they sold him.

Maimonides defines repentance as follows:

> What constitutes complete repentance? He who is confronted by the identical situation wherein he previously sinned, and it lies within his power to commit the sin again, but he nevertheless abstains and does not succumb because he wishes to repent …this is a true penitent.[4]

Aware of how terribly guilty the brothers will feel once he reveals himself, Yosef needs to create a situation that would preempt this possibility. He must set up a scenario that will once again incite hatred for one of the brothers, and it must again be Yaakov's youngest and favorite child. This can only be Binyamin. Indeed, it is *he* who satisfies all the requirements needed to bring about a serious dispute among the brothers. And so Yosef sets Binyamin apart, making sure he is guilty of getting all the brothers into trouble — due to the discovery of the cup and the money in his sack, which he seemingly stole[5] — and favoring him, just as

---

4. *Mishne Torah,* Hilchot Teshuvah 2:1.
5. *Bereshit* 44:12.

their father Yaakov, favored Yosef many years earlier.[6] This gives the brothers good reason to hate Binyamin and to abandon him. It is the ultimate test. Will they let their little brother down, or will they fight for him and not sell him to the enemy?

If they choose the latter, they will finally gain peace of mind; once Yosef reveals himself, there will no longer be need for feelings of guilt. They will know that they have repented! They have uprooted their earlier behavior in an optimal way.

In doing all this, Yosef satisfies the need of his own subconscious to take revenge, and also allows his brothers to believe that he *had* his revenge, while presenting them with the opportunity to do *teshuvah*. All of this is accomplished in one brilliant move, carefully planned and executed.

What Yosef doesn't realize is that the plan may not entirely work. What if the brothers don't believe that after he has had his "revenge" he will no longer consider them guilty and all will be well? Perhaps he will continue to take revenge now that Yaakov is no longer alive! And indeed this *is* what the brothers seem to believe. It creates an enormous dilemma for Yosef. How will he convince them that such is not the case? If he can't persuade them of his sincere belief that there is no place for vengeance, then there is no chance that his relationship with them will, once and for all, be healed. The only thing he *might* be able to convince them of is that he won't take revenge *in deed*. But he realizes that he can't prove to them that he doesn't bear a grudge. They won't believe him.

Turning the tables

Again, he makes a smart move. Instead of trying to convince them of what they believe is impossible, he asks them: What about you? Don't you have reason to bear a grudge against *me* even after all you have done to me? Perhaps you were right in

---

6. Ibid. 37:3-4.

your animosity toward me. After all, my behavior was obnoxious. I spoke evil about you to our father.[7] My dreams that you would bow down to me obviously distressed you. Who would not be upset? I understand that you felt mistreated when our father gave the many-colored garment to me and not to any of you. In many ways, I laid the trap that ensnared you. So why put all the guilt on yourselves? *We are all guilty.* Perhaps I made your lives as miserable as you made mine. More than that, I know that you were looking for me when you came to Egypt. You didn't come only to buy food, but also to find me and make peace with me. But I didn't want you to have the satisfaction of finding me, so I set the stage — threatening you, putting our brother Shimon in jail and causing you enormous problems when dealing with our youngest brother, Binyamin.

Are we not even, then? I live a life of wealth. I have servants at my beck and call. I am second in power — probably not only in Egypt, since Egypt is by far the largest empire in the world. So who has more reason to complain, *you or me?* You had to suffer through a terrible famine and live day and night with a depressed father, while I enjoyed myself as the spoiled second monarch of Egypt.

Is it not remarkable that you tried to harm me, but it only partially succeeded? Events turned in a way that nobody could have expected. Your "terrible" deeds were actually instrumental in my becoming who I am today: a wealthy and powerful man, enjoying his life as few can. So why should I take revenge on you? It is *you* who have good reason to take revenge on me! You have made me a great, powerful and wealthy man. But what have I done for you all these years? I left you out in the cold, never stretching out my hand to you in the Land of Israel. I never tried to make contact with you and our father; and we would never have met had you not taken the initiative. It was not *I* who searched for

---

7. Ibid. 37:2; See also Rashi.

you. I would have let you die in the famine! Is that not as bad as what you did to me? In fact, it is much worse!

So, I should be thankful to you for what you did to me, even if the beginnings were difficult. Not only that: I wonder why you don't want to take revenge on me *now*, now that you stand in front of me! I am most vulnerable. You could shout at me, injure me, and even kill me. There are no servants here; I sent them all away to ensure that we would be alone!

Don't you realize what outstanding tzaddikim you are? I am by far inferior to you! Because of what you did to me I can save our nation. So it is not I who is to be praised; it is *you* who brought all this about. Looking even deeper, there is no explanation for this surreal story but that God engineered it, and no one else.

Arguing this way, Yosef not only convinces his *brothers* of their blamelessness, but he achieves his ultimate goal: convincing his own subconscious. By planning this whole strategy and contending that it is not he who should be upset but his brothers, it becomes clear that there is absolutely no place for revenge.

Revenge? I don't know what you're talking about! Not only will I not take revenge on you; I cannot even bear a grudge against you.

This is the ingenious wisdom that Yosef demonstrates. He argues against himself and convinces himself that there is only One Who is behind this story, and that personal feelings have no part in this.

He achieves closure on all levels.

Questions to Ponder
from the DCA Think Tank

1. The question of strategies to promote healing and growth for victims of violence and abuse is, sadly, as relevant as ever in our modern world. Yosef's strategy, in Rabbi Cardozo's account, is one that seeks healing for the victim (Yosef), the perpetrators (the brothers) and their relationship. It involves acknowledgment of his pain and vulnerability as well as understanding and empathy for the perpetrators. That is a tall order, and it is noteworthy that Yosef does this when he is no longer in a position of risk vis-e-vis his brothers. In our modern world, are there circumstances where this strategy of mutual healing is appropriate (for example, family mediation or therapy)? Are there circumstances where it is inappropriate?

2. In Rabbi Cardozo's account, revenge does not work and is even counter-productive, since it leads to an escalating spiral of violence such as blood feuds. Is there a place for revenge in maintaining the moral equilibrium of civilization? Societies, for example, solve the problem of the escalating spiral by taking punishment out of the hands of the victim and placing it in the hands of an independent penal system. Is revenge the (or an) underlying principle of the concept of punishment?

3. Yosef understood his suffering as also giving rise to the circumstances that enabled him to affect great good in the world, primarily to save his family, the future nation. It was in this way that he perceived God's hand in his fate. Our modern world, too, has its moral heroes for whom great suffering and tragedy has been a springboard for doing good in the world. Is this Judaism's alternative to the project of theodicy—that of justifying God in the face of the existence of evil?

Vayechi

The Great Educational Challenge

> וישלח ישראל את ימינו וישת על ראש
> אפרים והוא הצעיר ואת שמאלו על ראש
> מנשה שכל את ידיו כי מנשה הבכור
>
> Yisrael stretched out his right hand and placed
> [it] on Ephraim's head, although he was the
> younger, and his left hand [he placed] on
> Menashe's head. He guided his hands deliberately,
> for Menashe was the firstborn. *Bereshit 48:14*

A PERSON CAN know with certainty that he succeeded in educating his children only when he sees the conduct of his grandchildren. And even then one cannot be entirely sure.

In the story of Yaakov's struggles with his children's upbringing, the Torah, in a most consistent fashion, alerts us to the extreme difficulty of successful parenting. In particular, the way he handled his sons' delicate relationships is a source of considerable controversy.[1] After demonstrating a greater level of love and devotion to his son Yosef, the brothers became embroiled in a major rift, which ultimately led to one of the great tragedies in Jewish history — the enslavement of the people of Israel in Egypt for 210 years.

One would readily be able to forgive Yaakov for making this mistake if the root of the problem lay in his relative inexperience

---

1. *Bereshit 37.*

in the field of education. But if that were the case, why then did he make the same mistake when dealing with his grandchildren? Why did he openly favor Yosef's children over the children of his other sons? Indeed, Yaakov only seems interested in Yosef's sons, Ephraim and Menashe. We never read a single word about the other brothers' sons,[2] nor do we hear anything about Yaakov's relationships with them. This complete silence is telling. Yaakov seems to have given time and attention only to Ephraim and Menashe. Only with *them* did he converse. Even more astonishing is the fact that they were the only grandchildren who received Yaakov's special blessings before he died.

As if this were not enough blatant favoritism, Yaakov openly favored one of Yosef's sons over the other! When blessing Ephraim and Menashe, Yaakov went out of his way to bless the younger (Ephraim) before the older (Menashe)![3] Did he not remember the disastrous consequences of showing this sort of bias in front of his own sons? Should he not have learned his lesson by now? No longer can we excuse Yaakov's behavior as youthful inexperience and indiscretion!

Suffering and Blossoming

Rabbi Yaakov Kamenetsky, in his monumental work *Emet Le-Yaakov*,[4] calls our attention to the difference between the names that Yosef gave his two sons. Both, as is well known, were born in Egypt. When the oldest was born, Yosef called him Menashe, *ki nashani Elokim*.[5] Rabbi Samson Rafael Hirsch translates this verse as, "because God has made my trouble and all my paternal house into creditors to me." When his second son was born, Yosef

---

2. With the exception of Yehuda's two sons who died.
3. *Bereshit* 48:13-20.
4. See *Emet Le-Yaakov* on *Bereshit* 41:51, 48:5.
5. Ibid. 41:51.

named him Ephraim, "because God has made me blossom (*ki hifrani Elokim*) in the land of my affliction."⁶

There is a remarkable difference between these two names. When naming Menashe, Yosef made reference to the pain of living in a foreign country, with strong feelings of nostalgia for his father's house. Although he thrived in, and even ruled, his foreign home, his whole personality objected and rebelled against Egypt's idolatrous culture. He refused to take part in it, however deeply involved he became in its governmental administration. By the time Yosef had to choose a name for his second son Ephraim, however, it seems that some kind of metamorphosis had taken place within him. While he was still aware of his unusual position as an Israelite in a strange land, he had somehow come to feel more comfortable in his new home. "God has made me blossom in the land of my affliction."⁷

The distinction is most telling. While there is little doubt that Yosef remained, throughout all his life, first and foremost an Israelite, the hostile climate of Egypt obviously exerted an influence. Yosef had to adapt himself, at least externally, to survive and succeed in his new environment, and this must have played a role in shaping his ultimate identity. Often, a person remains unaware of slight changes taking place within his personality. Assimilation is a slow and, at the start, unrecognizable process. It is only when others make us aware, that we realize what we have become.

From this perspective Yaakov's choices as a grandfather become more comprehensible. Ephraim and Menashe were the only two grandchildren who were not born and raised in close proximity to Yaakov. While the other grandchildren grew up in Yaakov's home, nurtured by the land of Israel, Ephraim and Menashe

---

6. Ibid. 41:52.
7. See *Emet Le-Yaakov* that this can also be seen from the fact that Ephraim is not so much a Jewish as an Egyptian name. It is similar to the words, Pharaoh, Potifar, Shifra and Puah.

came of age in a foreign country and never got to experience their grandfather and the nurturing environment of his thoroughly "Jewish" home.

Surely this must have worried Yaakov greatly. The question of how these grandchildren would maintain their "Jewish" identities in such spiritually hostile surroundings must have been on his mind constantly. Yaakov therefore proclaims to Yosef, "Now your sons who were born to you in the land of Egypt before I came to you in Egypt, are mine; Ephraim and Menashe shall be mine like Reuven and Shimon."[8] In other words, I will have to draw them back into the family before they are lost.

This interpretation, however, does not explain why he favored Ephraim over Menashe.

By looking beneath the surface, we can conclude that there must have been a major difference in the education these two sons received. By the time Ephraim was born, Yosef, not yet fully involved with the administration of Egypt and still more of a foreigner, had already made an indelible mark on his son Menashe's young psyche. Surely Yosef communicated clearly that, *although I am the second ruler in this country, always remember that this does not affect my loyalty towards my God and my people. We are first and foremost Israelites.*

But by the time Ephraim was born, Yosef's feelings of being a foreigner had faded somewhat; and without the constant reinforcement of a strong and unwavering message of Jewish identification, his younger son's development was necessarily more vulnerable to external influences.[9]

---

8. *Bereshit* 48.

9. According to this interpretation, some extended time must have passed between the births of the two brothers, which is unclear in the text.

Susceptibility

As such, Yaakov was right to worry more about Ephraim's spiritual training than Menashe's. He knew that Ephraim was much more susceptible to the *"kulturgesellschaft"* (cultural society) of Egypt, having grown up in the sweet but toxic atmosphere of Pharaoh's palace. It was therefore necessary, for the sake of the future of the Jewish people, for Yaakov to give more time to Ephraim than to Menashe. He needed to instill in him "Jewish" values and to uproot the negative influences from his childhood. Menashe, by contrast, came from a relatively stronger "Jewish" background and hence needed less special attention. Clearly this was even more the case for the rest of his grandchildren, all of whom were born in the land of Israel and raised on Yaakov's knees. No doubt, all of them were well-aware of their assimilated cousin's precarious situation, and may have even have encouraged Yaakov to give Ephraim more of his time and attention.

This could also explain why Yaakov placed his right hand on Ephraim's head, and gave him a stronger blessing than his older brother. Since he was more exposed to the culture of Egypt, he and his descendants would need a greater level of encouragement and Divine assistance. In taking this approach, we see that Yaakov in fact, did *not* repeat the mistake of favoring one child over another without specific cause and proper reason.

Most interesting is the fact that the child who suffered more from exposure to external influences was destined to overtake his brother, who received a much better "Jewish" education. Yaakov explicitly states about Menashe that, "He will also become a people, and he also will be great, nevertheless, his younger brother will be greater than he, and his seed shall become full to the nations." [10]

This is indeed a remarkable turnaround. Why should the child who was more exposed to the secular world have a brighter future

---

10. *Bereshit* 48:19.

than the one who received a much stronger and more traditional education?

In fact, this also seems to be the case with Moshe Rabbenu, who was raised by a non-Jewish mother and educated in Pharaoh's palace, and nevertheless grew up to become the greatest Jew in history, as well as the greatest Jewish prophet and leader. Were there no better candidates? Perhaps someone blessed with a proper Jewish education? Why select an assimilated Jewish boy, who may not have even known that he was an Israelite until later in life?

Courage and strength

The answer is that a person who has to fight for his Jewish identity will, in the end, have more courage and strength to stand up to outside influences precisely because he has participated in, and gained a familiarity with, the outside world. Moshe was the ideal leader *because* he was raised in a culture that opposed Jewish values and thus had to prove and build his character through many inner spiritual battles.

Looking into the blessing that Yaakov gave to Ephraim, we encounter a similar idea. Yaakov tells him that he will "become full to the nations." While there exist many possible explanations for this unusual expression, we may suggest that Ephraim's tribe would, more than any other, possess the power to stand strong against the forces of assimilation. Rashi clearly alludes to this in his commentary when he writes, "All the world will be filled with the glory [of Yehoshua who was a descendant of Ephraim] when his fame and his name will go forth...."[11]

It is most revealing that Jewish parents have, since ancient times, blessed their children with the blessing suggested by Yaakov Avinu: "With you shall Israel bless, saying: May God make you

---

11. Ad loc.

as Ephraim and Menashe."[12]

Yaakov's blessing expresses the delicate balance between the need for a strong "Jewish" identity and the capacity to interact with the outside world. Finding this middle path is far from easy, and trying to do so has been a source of constant problems throughout Jewish history. Too much introversion leads to dangerous isolation, because it soon becomes impossible to relate to the greater community of human beings, which in turn prevents us from fulfilling our function as a "light unto the nations." Too much adaptation, however, brings with it an essential loss of identity which leads inevitably to assimilation and devastation. To locate the right equilibrium requires a special blessing indeed, and this is precisely what we hope for our children when we bless them with the words of Yaakov Avinu, grandfather *par excellence*.

Questions to Ponder
from the DCA Think Tank

1. Rabbi Cardozo presents the non-Jewish environment in which Ephraim and Menashe (and Moshe) grew up as uniformly negative. The only advantage of growing up in such an environment is that it presented a test of character, and those who pass the test and resist the outside influences are thereby strengthened. Do you think this is the only benefit of being exposed to non-Jewish culture and the "greater community of human beings" or are there positive benefits too? If so, what do you think are the positive benefits of such exposure?

---

12. *Bereshit* 48:20.

2. If growing up in a non-Jewish environment is a test of character, there is a risk that only the exceptional few will pass the test; a select few will rise to greatness but many will be lost to assimilation. Is there an argument, then, for saying that Jewish communities should close themselves off as much as possible from their outside environment?

3. If closing oneself off from the non-Jewish environment is not a realistic possibility, what are the educational challenges that follow from this? What kind of Jewish education offers the best hope for sustaining a strong Jewish identity and commitment in the face of pressure to assimilate? Should children attending Jewish schools be shielded from potentially controversial topics (for example, issues of sexual identity) or should these be confronted head on? Are there issues of age-appropriateness? What other features of Jewish education are essential for instilling a strong Jewish identity and commitment?

4. In what ways do you think the Jewish people and the State of Israel are, or could be, a "light unto the nations" in the modern world? Do you think the Jewish people today gives sufficient attention to its role as a "light unto the nations"? If yes, what are some specific ways in which this idea manifests itself? If no, how do you think Jewish practice would or should change if it were to take seriously the Jewish responsibility to be a "light unto the nations"?

The Number of the Generations before Him[1]

> ועתה שני בניך הנולדים לך בארץ מצרים
> עד באי אליך מצרימה לי הם אפרים
> ומנשה כראובן ושמעון יהיו לי
>
> Now, your two sons, who were born to you in the land of Egypt before I came to you in Egypt, shall be mine; Ephraim and Menashe shall be mine no less than Reuven and Shimon. *Bereshit 48:5*

THE MISHNA IN Eduyot (2:9) makes the following observation in the name of Rabbi Akiva:

> A father endows his son with comely appearance, strength, riches, wisdom, longevity and *"mispar hadoroth lefanav"* (the number of generations before him). And this is the secret of redemption, as it says, "He proclaimed the generations from the beginning." (Isaiah 41.1)

There is indeed a lot of evidence that the genetic code affects the child's physical appearance and intellectual capacity. In addition, economic and other circumstances, together with the environment at home, influence much of the child's future. But what is meant by: "mispar hadoroth lefanav?"

In our day and age, it is becoming harder and harder for different

---

1. Inspired by the writings of Rabbi Joseph B. Solovietchik.

generations to communicate. The radical changes which are taking place in technology and science, together with major changes in outlook make it nearly impossible for parents and children to speak the same language. The generation gap widens all the time; we can foresee a day when parents and children will relate to each other as complete strangers.

Jews, as no other nation, have been confronted with this problem. Our nearly 4,000 year history has constantly reminded us of the danger of our children losing interest and commitment to our common heritage. Avraham has difficulties in conveying his mission to his son Yishmael; Yitshak has great problems in getting his message across to his two sons, Yaakov and Esav. Yaakov himself does not seem to escape this problem either, and becomes the unintentional initiator of a lot of bitterness between his children, because he seems to favor one over the others.

In all these cases, it is misapprehension that causes the problem. Words and even body language and gestures take on new forms and meanings. This can be clearly demonstrated in the case of the "many colored garment" which Yaakov gave to Yosef. According to Malbim, this garment was given to Yosef with the explicit purpose of being used only when serving his old father (Yosef was the only one at home). In no way was the intention to show any favor to Yosef. The brothers' mindset, however, was such that they were not able to grasp this and consequently they misread the situation with disastrous consequences. The cultural environment in which the brothers operated, i.e. the society at large, had by now given a different meaning to this kind of gesture.

In exactly the same way, parents today experience great frustration when they suddenly realize that their children completely misunderstand them because they translate their parents' words into a foreign context (and so vice versa).

There seems to be only one way in which we can overcome this problem: by creating a psychological language that delves deeper than the general cultural and sociological environment in which children find themselves. Human beings are indeed deeply influenced by their surroundings, but, on a deeper level, they seem to carry a kind of psychological gene which can create bridges spanning many generations.[2] This may be what Carl Gustaf Jung meant when he spoke of the archetype, a kind of a primordial mental image which keeps recurring in a nation and envelopes us psychologically in our natural religious inner life. Whatever this "gene" may consist of, it will have a real effect only when it is constantly re-activated and relived. This is done by making sure that the past does not become outdated; if anything, it must be "fore-dated."

And here we discover the purpose of Jewish learning and practice. Jews do not study the past because of what *happened*, but because of what *is happening* and what *will happen*.

In Jewish education, Avraham is not a mythical figure, but an ever present inspiration. We experience his tribulations and his wanderings ourselves. We travel with him to Canaan and we tremble when we stand with him on the mountain where he is about to sacrifice Yitshak. We escape with Yaakov, and we share the prison cell with Yosef and stand next to him when he is appointed second in command of Egypt. We lead the Jews in the wilderness together with Moshe and compose the psalms together with King David. Slowly we enter into a world with its own language, we share in the solemnities of the "great ones," dream their dreams and become their companions. Here, there is no longer a generation gap but a "fraternity of the committed"[3] which overcomes all the

---

2. Jung introduced the term "collective unconscious," as different from the "personal unconscious." He wrote: "The collective unconscious, therefore, as the ancestral heritage of possibilities of representation, is not individual but common to all men." *The Structure and Dynamics of the Psyche* (New York: Pantheon Books, 1960) p. 152.

3. A phrase used by Rabbi Joseph B. Soloveitchik in a talk delivered on March 20, 1974, as quoted by Aaron Rakeffet-Rothkoff in *The Rav: The World of Rabbi Joseph B. Soloveitchik*, Ktav Publishing House, Inc., 1999, p. 186.

superficial pressures and external pulls of society.

This explains why Yaakov seems to relate much better to his grandchildren than to his own children. He establishes a most remarkable communication with Ephraim and Menashe. There are no tensions and no jealousy. He literally bridges the generation gap when he declares to Yosef, "Now your two sons, who were born to you in the land of Egypt before I came to you in Egypt, are mine. Ephraim and Menashe shall be mine, like Reuven and Shimon."[4] He blesses them, learns with them and no doubt must have played with them. Indeed Yaakov is called Yisrael Sava, "Israel the old one" which may also mean Yaakov the definitive grandfather.[5]

Why does he relate better to his grandchildren than to his children? I suggest that this is due to the fact that it is only at an older age that he meets his grandchildren. His trials, tribulations and his life experience have made him into a man of great wisdom. He has learned from the mistakes of youth and inexperience. Now, in his old age, he has developed into a well-balanced person, and it is under these conditions that he meets his grandchildren. The tranquility which he now experiences makes him into a great educator. This he was not able to offer to his children, however much loved all of them.

For this reason he could not have the same impact on his children as he had, years later, on his grandchildren. His children still saw him in his "raw" state, while his grandchildren saw him as a refined and highly distinguished personality. In this way, he became not only the unique grandfather and educator but he fulfilled the mishnaic statement of "mispar hadoroth lefanav"; he connected the later generations with the earlier ones in an unusual covenant of fraternity. The limitations of time were replaced with the power of eternity. Not for nothing does the Jewish tradition require parents to bless their children with the blessing of

---

4. Bereshit 48.5
5. Bereshit Rabbah 70.1

a grandfather. It is indeed the secret of the Redemption.

Questions to Ponder
from the DCA Think Tank

1. Is it possible that Ephraim and Menashe, having an additional degree of separation from Yaakov, find it easier to relate to him because he is a more abstract figure, and relate to him on their own terms instead of the more direct way a child relates to their parent? Similarly, could looking back at Avraham provide that same benefit of abstractness, as an opportunity to hold a mirror up to our own life story, with the added closeness of knowing that his story is mine as well?

2. Has there actually ever been a change in communication and understanding between parents and children? Could there be a spectrum of variation? What differences children with immigrant parents experience, who don't use the same language to communicate? For example, a Farsi speaker moving to an English speaking country, and having English speaking children.

Glossary

Books of the Hebrew Bible

Bereshit: "At the beginning." Genesis

Shemot: "Names." Exodus

Vayikra: "He called" Leviticus

Bamidbar: "In the desert." Numbers,

Devarim: "Words." Deuteronomy

Hebrew terms

Aggadah: Interpretive story, usually based on a Biblical text.

Aguna: "Chained." A woman who, for whatever reason, has been unable to receive from her husband a valid bill of divorces, and is thus not free to remarry.

Akedah: "Binding." Generally used to refer to Avraham's binding of Isaac, in fulfillment of the divine command to sacrifice his son.

Am Segulah: A treasured people. Often mistranslated as "chosen people".

Am Yisrael: The People of Israel.

Am Kadosh: A "Holy People". The phrase appears in the Torah in the context of the commandment to the newly-liberated Children of Israel to hold themselves to a higher standard than that of the societies around them.

Aravit: The evening prayer.

Aron Kodesh: The Ark in which the Torah is kept in a synagogue.

Ashkenazim: Jews from central and eastern Europe, as opposed to Sepharadim, referring to Spanish and some North African Jews.

Avodah: "Service." Used to refer both to worship and to work, as in Avodat Hashem, serving God.

Bet Knesset: (plural: *batei knesset*) Synagogue, House of Assembly.

Bet Midrash: House of study (of Torah).

Brachah: (plural: Brachot): Blessing. Usually refers to a short blessing of gratitude before eating or before performing a Mitzvah.

Counting the Omer: The verbal counting of each of the forty-nine days between the holidays of Passover and Shavuot, mandated by Leviticus 23:15–16.

Eretz Yisrael: The Land of Israel.

Gemara: The part of the Talmud which comprises commentary on the primary code of Jewish law, the Mishnah.

Get: Bill of divorce.

Glossary

Halachah: (plural: *Halachot*) Often defined as "Jewish Law", it actually encompasses the entire body of Jewish culture, tradition, and philosophy.

Hallel: A compilation of psalms of praise recited at special occasions throughout the Jewish year.

Hashem: "The Name." The substitution in text or speech for the four-letter name of God, which, written out, is called the *Shem HaMeforash* (the Explicit Name).

Havdalah: Ceremony at the end of Shabbat that separates the sacred time from the mundane workaday week.

Hester Panim: "Hiding of the Face (of God)". A term used in Deuteronomy to refer to a period of history when the Jews will be made to feel the complete absence of God.

Kapparah: Atonement.

Kashrut: Jewish dietary laws.

Kiddush: "Sanctification." A brief ceremony involving a blessing over wine to introduce the Sabbath and other festivals.

Kiddush Hashem: (opposite: *Hillul Hashem*) "Sanctification of the Name." Any action by which a Jew acts as an ambassador of God by behaving in a way that brings honor to God in the eyes of others.

Kippah: A special cap traditionally worn by Jewish men.

Kohelet: Ecclesiastes, a book of wisdom literature attributed to King Solomon.

Kohen: (plural: *kohanim*) Priest, A male descendant of Aharon (Aaron), the brother of Moses.

Mashiach: "Anointed." A descendant of the House of David, who according to Jewish tradition is prophesied to re-establish Jewish sovereignty in the Land of Israel and bring back the exiles.

Mezuzah: A parchment contained in a decorative case and inscribed with specific Hebrew verses from the Torah. These verses include the Jewish "declaration of faith" — Shema Yisrael. A Mezuzah is affixed to the door post of each room in a Jewish home.

Midrash: "Explanation." An expounding that brings out the deeper meaning of a text or of a Halachah. Midrashim are typically stories that are not meant to be taken literally, but which use evocative imagery to paint a picture in the mind of the listener.

Mikveh: Ritual bath used for purification.

Minhah: The afternoon prayer.

Mitzvah: (plural: mitzvot, Commandment): Any action undertaken in accordance with God's will, including acts of kindness.

Neshama: Higher soul.

Nefesh: The embodied soul, or life force.

Olam HaBa: "The Next World." The afterlife.

P'shat: The simple meaning of the text, as opposed to the deeper levels.

Glossary

Shabbat: The Jewish Sabbath, which begins shortly before sundown on Friday evening and lasts until after sunset on Saturday night. During Shabbat, Jews cease all actions that involve willful, conscious creation. The day is traditionally spent with family and friends.

Shaharit: The morning prayer.

Sh'chinah: "The Presence." Often referred to as the feminine aspect of God.

Shema Yisrael: The fundamental statement of Jewish loyalty to God: "Hear, O Israel, the Eternal (is) our God, the Eternal is one." It is recited twice daily, and is traditionally also recited in the last moments before death.

Sh'losh Esre Ikarim: Thirteen Principles of the Rambam, considered by some to be the core beliefs and worldviews of Judaism.

Shoah: The Holocaust.

Siddur: (plural: *Siddurim*) Prayer book.

Slichot: Penitential poems and prayers, especially those said in the period leading up to the High Holidays, and on fast days.

Tallit: Prayer shawl — a four-cornered garment to which are attached Tzitzit, specially tied fringes.

The Talmud: A compilation of what used to be the Oral Law, including the *Mishna* and the *Gemara*. It is second only to the Bible in terms of its importance in Judaism.

Tehillim: Psalms. A collection of songs and poems, some of which date back to the Kingdom of David.

T'fillah: Prayer. In Jewish traditional texts, it refers to the central prayer of Judaism, which is performed three times a day. Also known as the Shmonah Esre (Eighteen Benedictions), or the Amida (Standing Prayer).

Tikvah: Hope.

The Torah: This term may refer specifically to the first Five Books of Moses in the Bible (the Pentateuch), or to the entire set of laws, written and oral, that we believe we received at Mount Sinai, and the vast literature of commentary and interpretation surrounding those laws.

T'shuvah: "Return." The process of repentance and rehabilitation from wrong-doing.

Tsaddik: Righteous person.

Tzitzit: Specially knotted ritual fringes that are attached to each corner of a four-cornered garment, which religious Jews wear under their shirts. See *Bamidbar* 15:38-40.

Viddui: The verbal confession of wrong-doing that accompanies the process of T'shuvah.

Acknowledgments

Rabbi Moshe Benzaquen
Amy Bernstein
Bettina and Joe Blanga
David and Nelly Blanga
Family Marc Blanga
Gerald and Naomi Braunstein
Sid and Judy Tenenbaum-Cardozo
Edward and Orna Cohen
Micha and Cilly Eitje
Family Michael Feldmar
Sharon and Eli Gindi
Joseph and Leelah Gitler
Wim and Gerry van der Hoek
Shimmy and Pearl Lopian
Michael and Hilla Kagan
Michael and Judith Kaiser
Eefje and Eddy Wolff van der Kar
Dr. David Katzin
Terrence Klingman
Jonathan and Tamar Koschitzky

Larry Kraus
Ellie and Marshall Jaffe-Kulman
Moshe and Elishva (z.l.) Moskovits
Dr. David and Marcia Nimmer
Avraham and Caroline (z.l) Packter
Louise and Menno Paktor
Family Cohen Paraira
Family Michael Pereira
Eliahoe and Haddasa Philipson
Gerry and Katy Polak
Doron and Sharon Sanders
Joop and Evelyne Sanders-Al-Falk
Family Joey Shamah
Alex and Marguerite Schottland
Yudit Sidikman
David Suissa
Caroline and Daniel Tamman
Dr. Jaap N. Velleman
Charles and Ariella Zeloof
David Zeloof

About the Author

Nathan Lopes Cardozo (b. 1946), hailing from the Portuguese-Spanish Jewish community in Amsterdam, is a philosopher, New Age halachist, author of 13 books, and lecturer in Jewish communities, yeshivot and universities in Israel and abroad. He studied for 12 years in Ultra Orthodox yeshivot but, after intensive studies in Jewish and general philosophy, carved out his own unprecedented approach to understanding Judaism. He is the founder and dean of the David Cardozo Academy in Jerusalem and its think tank, which focus on finding new halachic and philosophical approaches to dealing with the crisis of religion and identity among Jews and non-Jews, including in the State of Israel. Rabbi Cardozo is known for his originality and fearlessness when presenting his controversial insights into Judaism. His ideas are widely debated internationally via books and social media.

Authors of Questions to Ponder

Anne Gordon
Calev ben Dor
Jay Gutovich
Yehoshua Looks
Dina Pinner
Jonathan Rossner
Elliot Sacks
Yael Shahar
Yael Valier
Yael Unterman
Shoshana Michael Zucker

www.ingramcontent.com/pod-product-compliance
Lightning Source LLC
Chambersburg PA
CBHW030112240426
43673CB00002B/50